MW01277646

The Ultimate Linux Guide for Hackers

2021 Edition

□ **Copyright 2021- All rights reserved.**

This book is copywritten and no part of this book may be copied, reproduced, shared or kept in any form or any means be it electronically, photocopying, scanning without express written permission from the Copywriters or permission through purchasing a copy of the book.

Limit of Liability:

The distributor and the book author make no portrayals or guarantees concerning the exactness or culmination of the substance of this work and explicitly disavow all guarantees, including without restriction guarantees of readiness for a specific reason. No guarantee might be made or stretched out by deals or limited time materials. The exhortation and procedures contained thus may not be appropriate for each circumstance. This work is sold with the understanding that the distributor isn't occupied with rendering lawful, bookkeeping, or other expert administrations. In the event that expert help is required, the administrations of an able expert individual ought to be looked for. Neither the distributor nor the writer will be at risk for harms emerging here from. The way that an association or Web webpage is alluded to in this work as a reference as well as a potential wellspring of additional data does not imply that the author or the distributor embraces the data the association or site may give or suggestions it might make. Further, readers ought to know that Internet sites recorded in this work may have changed or vanished between when this work was written and when it is read.

Disclaimer

This book was written specifically for training reasons only. It does not legitimize certain aspects like hacking which can be illegal in different parts of the world in accordance with applicable law and organizational policies. There is no legal authorization for what can be considered legal in this book. Prior to taking their own decisions, the readers should review their privacy policies, organizational policies and the laws of their country of origin and residence. In any case, they cannot rely on this publication as a defense if they make any violations. The author is not liable for any actions which can be taken by a reader based on this publication and is not liable for any actions which might be taken after reading the publication.

Table of Contents

Preface

Linux is the most dominant hacking operating system in the world. This operating has a number of distributions that are built specifically for hacking and security. The Linux operating system is utilized in many areas of computer security ranging from vulnerability assessments to penetration testing.

The Linux operating system distributions that are meant for hacking and security come pre-packaged with over 100 hacking tools. These distributions like any other Linux computer have the all-powerful bash shell; which is the most powerful and pliant way of interacting with the operating system kernel and attendant services. A Linux shell is used to execute individual commands. Commands are a set of instructions sent to the Linux kernel to tell the computer what to do. The Linux shell can also execute and interpret commands from a written text file called a bash script, which enables easy automation of tasks. For all expert Linux users and those interested in computer security and forensics, the command line or shell gives unprecedented power to the hacker.

Introduction

Purpose

This book is a comprehensive guide to aimed to teach Linux system administrators how to hack information technology systems to find their vulnerabilities before mischievous and evil attackers do. The book is an introduction to using the Linux operating system to hack. It is important to note that studying the most usual hacking and IT system attack methods and fostering the hacker mindset will help improve the security of information technology systems and help system administrators build more secure systems from the ground up.

Prerequisites

Experience

This book is designed for the beginner hacker or other budding IT professionals who want to learn how to use the Linux operating system's hacking tools. To work through this book well enough, the novice hacker must have a working knowledge of bash scripting, python scripting, Transmission Control Protocol/Internet Protocol (TCP/IP), Domain Naming System (DNS), HTTP, HTML, open-source databases and web servers like Apache and Nginx.

Hardware

To go through this book, learners are required to use a machine running either VirtualBox or VMware. The learner is also expected to install a Kali Linux virtual machine and a Metasploitable virtual machine prior to work through the content of this book.

Kali Linux can be downloaded from http://www.kali.org.

Metasploitable can be downloaded from: http://sourceforge.net/projects/metasploitable/files/Metasploitable2

The reader should ensure both machines are on the same virtual network and that both machines have Internet access.

Chapter One: Linux Basics - A Hacker's Introduction

There are a whole lot of questions from IT novices and experts alike as regards which operating system is great for hackers. In this book we will begin by pointing out that nearly every professional and expert hacker worth their name in the world has used and uses the Linux operating system. This book is going to focus mainly on ethical hacking. Most of the hacking tools that are available in this world are developed for and on Linux platforms. We have some outliers, nonetheless, including software like Metasploit, Cain and Abel, Zenmap and Havij that are programmed or ported for Windows operating system.

When Linux applications are created in Linux, they often lose some of their capacities when they are ported to the Windows operating system. Moreover, there are Linux built-in capacities that are merely not readily available on Windows. This is why most hacker tools are developed on and ONLY for Linux in most instances.

Why is Linux OS good for Hacking?

Linux for ethical hackers is designed for the sole purpose of ethical hacking using the Linux operating system. A couple of competencies are needed for hackers to approach hacking using Linux, because many systems they hack into are Linux devices and a big proportion of today's instruments are Linux based.

There are a number of reasons why hackers prefer to use the Linux operating system. We detail some of the reasons in the ensuing section.

Why Hackers prefer Linux?

In order to get acquainted with the entire array of ethical hacking technologies, it is imperative to have a grasp of the Linux OS. Yasser Ibrahim, a systems engineer said in his article on Quora: "You must understand the basics up to expert knowledge in Linux and learn the commands on the console, shell scripting, understand the kernel and how it functions and get a grasp of the Linux file system.

Linux is open-source

One of the major reasons why IT security enthusiasts and hackers alike choose Linux instead of Windows is the capability to control and customize the Linux source code. This should particularly be remembered today, when privacy issues are a problem for noteworthy companies.

We can audit Linux

We have access to all of the Linux operating system's source code to enable us to understand its internal working. We can audit the source code and see the possibilities to improve on the code, detect any bugs.

Gritty control

Through its customizable kernel, the Linux operating system permits us to code and automate some elements of the operating system quickly and effortlessly use scripting languages like BASH and Python.

Built-in Hacking tools

Linux operating system has a fair percentage of in-built hacking tools that are specifically meant for this space. Most hacking tools function better in Linux distributions than in any other OS. This is because it utilizes, scripting languages including BASH and Python, that are lightweight, and it simplifies the writing of minimal code that has a great impact. Currently, Ubuntu accounts for more than 90% of open hacking utilities.

Linux holds the future

Embedded systems are highly dependent on the Linux kernel because it is powerful and lightweight as computing technology continues to advance. Every day, more and more devices are hooked up to the internet, and users use the Internet of Things. Linux-based devices need web security.

The reasons given above contribute to the use of Linux for ethical hacking and security. The future of computing protection is in the hands of ethical hackers who audit and assess systems for vulnerabilities before they are exploited by malicious hackers.

Linux works well for Ethical hacking

Linux users are able to download and set up a Linux OS instance on their physical machine or they can install it in a virtualized infrastructure such as Oracle VirtualBox. There is a range of Linux distributions designed for ICT security experts, ethical hacking, system auditing, forensic analysis and system weakness assessments. The listing below displays the Linux distributions designed for hacking and that are most often used in hacking

Kali Linux OS

The Debian-grounded Kali Linux operating system was previously called Backtrack and is the most popular security and hacking Linux distribution in the world. We have a world-class security operating system in Kali Linux which is very dependable in penetration testing, ethical hacking, and system security audits. The system comes with a number of utility packages used for the hacking process. It is developed on Debian Linux and is managed, operated, and maintained by a business named Offensive Security It is made up of several hacker technologies that make it the most desirable and potent hacking distribution.

Black Arch Security Operating System

Black Arch is a security platform based on the Arch Linux OS distribution and is designed with more than two thousand three hundred (2,300) applications for hacking. Even though it has more built-in hacking tools than Kali, it's a pretty fresh venture right now. It's also less stable compared to Kali.

Parrot Hacking Operating System

Parrot Linux security operating system is a defense-focused Linux distribution founded on the Debian Linux that provides a range of programs and resources for penetration testing, computer forensics, reverse engineering, hacking, anonymity, confidentiality and cryptography. This particular product has a standard operating desktop interface called MATE. Frozenbox developed this Parrot security operating system.

Santoku Mobile Security Linux System

Santoku is a bootable Linux security distribution that was designed specifically for mobile devices. This security utility has tools meant for mobile phone forensics, vulnerability assessments and auditing. Santoku Linux comes with a built-in SDK framework, hardware drivers and tools that permit newly paired mobile devices to be auto-detected and set up. Santoku Mobile Security Linux is a completely open and free community supported project sponsored by NowSecure which sponsors key team members of the project and some resources for system implementation and integration. In a simple to use open-source project, Santoku is engaged with mobile device forensics, evaluation and security.

Hacking BackBox Linux

BackBox Security Linux Hacking OS is a very young security OS designed for system infiltration tests, security auditing and vulnerability assessments. The core purpose of using Backbox is to provide an independent, effective and reliable security and defense testing system. XFCE, the lightweight Graphical User Interface Manager, is used by BackBox. This OS contains the most relevant common security and system defense auditing utilities for penetration testers and security experts. The software package covers web application evaluation, network analysis, stress testing, forensic computer analysis, activity, paperwork and documentation.

Kali Linux is the most widely used of the Linux hacking operating system variants above. The main focus is Kali Linux, but Backbox and Santoku Linux are going to get a cursory look. Begin by downloading Kali Linux and learning how to use the software before you are comfortable enough to use it every day on Oracle VirtualBox.

In summary, you have to master a couple of basic Linux skills, Linux networking, basic shell, Perl and Python scripting skills and the usage Linux hacking distributions such as Backbox Linux, Cyborg Linux and the best distribution called Kali Linux to become a worthwhile hacker.

Linux and Bash Shell Basics

Linux, as an operating system that can be used by hackers, has a number of ways of getting around. The most important tool for every hacker is information and the ability to know and maneuver in a system.

To get around, users can use the man command to know much about the system

```
[ppeters@rad-srv ~]$ man <COMMAND>
```

For this book the reader needs to gain familiarity with Kali Linux distribution.

What is a Linux Distribution

Although often used as a title for the whole of the OS, Linux is the kernel's title, a component that controls the interaction between computers and end-user apps.

On the other hand, the Linux distribution expression refers to a complete operating system that is built over the Linux kernel, generally comprising an installed system and many applications that are either pre-installed or packaged easily.

Debian GNU / Linux is a standard, high-quality and stable distribution for Linux. Building on the Debian project's work, Kali Linux provides over 300 utility packages, all of them related particularly to IT security and penetration testing.

Debian is an open-source program that supplies multiple copies of the operating system and we frequently use the term distribution when we talk about testing the Debian stable or Debian testing distributions in a specific version. The same is true for Kali Linux, for instance, the Kali Rolling distribution.

The Linux Environment

This section of the book is an immersive journey into the fundamental concepts of Linux file systems. The Linux file system is a virtual grouping of files and directories on the hard disk of the operating system. This file structure is the manner in which the Linux files are identified, stored, accessed and edited on a disk or directory for storage; the way files are structured on the disk. Linux provides data in files and folders like any other operating system. In turn, the files are included in folders (a folder is a type of Linux file that may include other files and directories). A folder may comprise additional directories, resulting in a hierarchical arrangement. This hierarchical data structure is called the Linux file system.

A unified model of all storage in the system is provided by the Linux file system. A separate root directory for the file system is specified by a forward tap (/). Then there is a file and directory hierarchy. Filesystem components can reside in various physical media such as hard disk, computer and CD-ROM.

What is a Linux File system

Not only do files store information but they also allow applications to collaborate, allow access to hardware devices, display certain file directories, provide information points and link machines or virtually over the network. Within Linux and Unix systems, files are the key concept. Basically, everything is viewed as a file in Linux; pipes to other processes, the computer system software, and even directories and references or links to files. Virtual files even provide a user with kernel structure access.

In Linux, a file symbolizes a single object, whilst a file system defines the manner in which files are saved on Linux system media. Media comprises hard disks or floppy, USB Disks and DVD-ROMs, network interface cards, and the machine's RAM. Every file system category implements distinctive properties. Not all types of files can be mounted on any file system, nor does any form of file system support any media. Files on a Linux system have type-specific properties. It is a common property of all files that they have a collection of privileges that indicate the group they belong to and who owns them. We have numerous types of files namely regular files, directories, special device files, regular pipes, named pipes, sockets, hard links and soft links.

First, **Regular Files** are used to keep information on a Linux file system. These are the common type of files which are vessels to store permanent data. Secondly we have **Directories, which are essentially** a special type of file that stores other files. The main directory's purpose is to hold the file system hierarchy. Directories are essentially files containing a list of other files. We have a third type of file called **Special Device Files.** These are fundamentally Linux kernel interfaces to a device or piece of hardware equipment that is attached to your machine, whether directly or through external ports like the USB port. We have two classes of special device files in existence, namely the buffered device files and the unbuffered device files. The buffered special device files are termed **block device** files and the unbuffered ones are termed the **character device** files.

The fourth type of file is called a **Regular Pipe,** which is primarily an interrelationship between two Linux system processes. Within a program, they handle the same file within the framework, but there is no reference in the file system. Only if you want to create a program is this sort of file useful. Pipes are a simple way of connecting commands from a user level, providing an output from one program as the input to some other program. We also have **Named Pipes** which are similar to our standard physical pipes but are defined in the Linux file system. Named pipes are used to communicate between processes, but they can exist even without any processes accessing them.

Next up we have a **Socket** which is akin to regular pipes we discussed above and execute the same purpose. The distinction is that a socket is utilized to converse over a network. Next are **Hard Links** which are just a sequential entry in a Linux folder structure of an existing file. A hard link is a mirror copy of the original file in a Linux file system. A hard link is similar to a new name for the file. We lastly mention **Symbolic or soft Link which** is an actual link or pointer to the original file.

A file system is split into two sections, called the user information and metadata; the latter includes the name of the file, creation time, the time it was modified, the file's size and position in the hierarchy of directories.

A partition is an information container and, if desired, can span a whole hard drive.

There are distinct partitions that usually have only one file system on your hard drive. Your computer or server's disk drive can have separate directories that commonly comprise one file system, such as one file system that houses the root directory / or another that contains the directory/home.

The logic of maintaining and managing various storage processes is possible with one file system per partition.

All of the Linux files include hardware devices like DVD ROMs, USB drives and floppy drives. Everything in the Linux operating system is considered a file.

The Linux filesystem consists of several files and the directories; under the root folder /, the ls command below can show the listing of all files and directories under / directory:

```
[ppeters@rad-srv ~]$ ls /
```

The command below is used to verify file and directory sizes and where they are mounted with:

```
[ppeters@rad-srv ~]$ df -h /
```

Linux File System Types

Linux Directory Structure

The Linux file system hierarchical structure has many directories that have certain purposes. Finding your path around Linux directories is simpler if you understand the function of specific directories. Another advantage of understanding how directories are typically used is that when you have a current environment, you can figure out where you can search for particular kinds of records. The Linux system folders are shortly described below:

The structure of the Linux OS system is divided into the folders below:

The /dev folder

The /dev directory is also called the Hardware Devices folder and it holds facts concerning all the hardware equipment attached to the file system.

This directory contains all the items dynamically generated by the **udev** system, on discovery by the Linux system during Power-on, Self-Test or when they are mounted.

The /var folder

The /var directory is a Linux folder or directory that holds files that are anticipated to be changing in size and content.

In most Linux distributions, log records are situated in /var/log file, and the /var/spool folder keeps the Linux printing queues.

The /bin directory

This encloses all the Linux executable binaries, critical system commands that are used in Linux single-user, and all the essential programs required by all system users.

The /sbin folder

The /sbin directory stores entirely less important system programs that run in the Linux single-user mode.

The /etc Linux folder

In Linux file systems, the /etc folder contains system settings and their configuration text files.

For instance, the file **/etc/resolv.conf** is a file that stores the IP addresses of the DNS servers that your system will use to resolve domain names to IP addresses.

The /lib folder

The /lib folder stores Linux system libraries commonly shared by application programs and that are mandatory for them to run.

The /boot folder

The Linux system /boot directory stores the files mandatory for booting.

The /opt folder

This is a Linux system directory also known as the Optional Directory which holds Linux software applications, that are set up and configured physically by the system administrator or user.

/tmp

This is the directory that contains temporary files that are removed from the system after every reboot.

/usr

This directory contains all the multi-tenant programs, utilities and data. This directory has the following common subdirectories:

- /usr/include: contains header files used to compile programs.

- usr/lib: contains libraries for programs in usr/(s)bin.

- usr/sbin: contains all the non-vital system binaries, such as system daemons. In modern Linux systems, this is actually connected symbolically to /sbin.

- usr/bin: this is the initial directory for executable commands of the system.

- usr/share: this is the shared data used by applications, generally architecture-independent.

- usr/src: this is the directory that holds the Kernel source code.

- usr/local: this directory holds all the information and commands exclusive to the resident device.

/dev Specials

This Specials directory contains all files delivered by the operating system that does not denote any physical device, but offer a way to access special features:

- /dev/null: this folder disregards everything written to it. It's convenient for discarding the unwanted output.

- /dev/zero: this folder contains an infinite number of zero bytes, which can be beneficial for generating files of a specified length.

- /dev/urandom and /dev/random these folders comprising of an infinite stream of operating-system-generated random numbers, accessible by all Linux program that wants to read them. The difference is that the second ensures a great opportunity and so it should be used for encoding, whereas the former can be used for matches..

The command below outputs random bytes in its result:

[ppeters@rad-srv ~]$ cat /dev/urandom | strings

The Linux Kernel

The Linux Kernel is the core or heart of the operating system responsible for managing input/output demands from software, and translates them into data processing instructions for the central processing unit (CPU).

To determine the Linux Kernel information, you can type the command below:

[ppeters@rad-srv root]$ cat /proc/version

Linux version 2.6.32-754.14.2.el6.x86_64 (mockbuild@x86-01.bsys.centos.org) (gcc version 4.4.7 20120313 (Red Hat 4.4.7-23) (GCC)) #1 SMP Tue May 14 19:35:42 UTC 2019

[ppeters@rad-srv root]$

We can pretty much print the related system information with the specific **uname** command. The flag **-a** means for all:

[ppeters@rad-srv root]$ uname -a

Linux rad-srv.uz.ac.zw 2.6.32-754.14.2.el6.x86_64 #1 SMP Tue May 14 19:35:42 UTC 2019 x86_64 x86_64 x86_64 GNU/Linux

[ppeters@rad-srv root]$

As an illustration below, we want to find out if we are using the up-to-date Linux Kernel on our server. The two commands below can be used to ascertain this and if they show a similar result then we know our Kernel is the newest version:

```
[ppeters@rad-srv root]$ rpm -qa kernel | sort -V | tail -n 1
```

```
[ppeters@rad-srv root]$ uname -r
```

The example output is below

```
[ppeters@rad-srv root]$ rpm -qa kernel | sort -V | tail -n 1
```

```
kernel-2.6.32-754.14.2.el6.x86_64
```

```
[ppeters@rad-srv root]$ uname -r
```

```
2.6.32-754.14.2.el6.x86_64
```

```
[ppeters@rad-srv root]$
```

Linux Processes

In the Linux Operating System, an executing program is termed a process. Each of the processes in Linux has an owner, who is the user currently logged in and is responsible for executing the program.

We can find out which programs or processes are running on the system using the **ps** command, also known as the process status command. The ps utility shows us the running processes' ID, also known as the PID or process ID. The Process ID is a distinctive lasting process identity and it is a fact that different copies of a given program will have separate PIDs.

In Linux we can choose if we want our processes to run either in the background or foreground. To put a job or process in the background we either run it with the & sign or we press the keyboard keys CTRL-Z and then type bg. To bring the job or process that is running in the background to the foreground, we use the fg utility. By typing fg in the terminal all processes in the background are brought to the forefront.

In Linux, we may want to see the listing of all processes not started from our existing session; to do this, we use the ps utility with the x switch as shown below:

```
[ppeters@rad-srv root]$ ps x
```

```
  PID TTY     STAT TIME COMMAND
```

```
17948 pts/0  S    0:00 bash
```

```
17988 pts/0  R+   0:00 ps x
```

```
[ppeters@rad-srv root]$
```

To view all your processes and those belonging to other users:

```
[ppeters@rad-srv root]$ ps aux
```

To show a listing of all the zombie processes you can do:

```
[ppeters@rad-srv root]$ ps aux | grep -w Z
```

```
ppeters 17993 0.0 0.0 103324 920 pts/0 S+ 20:54 0:00 grep -w Z
```

```
[ppeters@rad-srv root]$ ps -e
```

Top Utility

Linux has a very handy command called **top,** which is essentially a **table of processes**. It informs the user of which programs are using the most of memory or CPU:

```
[ppeters@rad-srv root]$ top
```

```
top - 20:57:29 up 37 days,  6:27,  1 user,  load average: 0.00, 0.00, 0.00
```

```
Tasks: 464 total,  1 running, 463 sleeping,  0 stopped,  0 zombie
```

```
Cpu(s): 0.0%us, 0.0%sy, 0.0%ni,100.0%id, 0.0%wa, 0.0%hi, 0.0%si, 0.0%st
```

```
Mem: 32877376k total, 1004576k used, 31872800k free, 194624k buffers
```

```
Swap: 4128764k total,    0k used, 4128764k free, 352112k cached
```

PID USER COMMAND	PR	NI	VIRT	RES	SHR	S	%CPU	%MEM	TIME+
17995 ppeters	20	0	15296	1556	948	R	0.7	0.0	0:00.07 top
84 root events/1	20	0	0	0	0	S	0.3	0.0	34:55.19
1 root init		20	0	19364	1560	1240	S	0.0	0.0	0:03.84
2 root kthreadd	20	0	0	0	0	S	0.0	0.0	0:00.02
3 root migration/0	RT	0	0	0	0	S	0.0	0.0	0:00.02
4 root ksoftirqd/0	20	0	0	0	0	S	0.0	0.0	0:00.14
5 root stopper/0	RT	0	0	0	0	S	0.0	0.0	0:00.00
6 root watchdog/0	RT	0	0	0	0	S	0.0	0.0	0:08.16
7 root migration/1	RT	0	0	0	0	S	0.0	0.0	0:00.30
8 root stopper/1	RT	0	0	0	0	S	0.0	0.0	0:00.00
9 root ksoftirqd/1	20	0	0	0	0	S	0.0	0.0	0:00.03
10 root watchdog/1	RT	0	0	0	0	S	0.0	0.0	0:06.95
11 root migration/2	RT	0	0	0	0	S	0.0	0.0	0:00.00
12 root stopper/2	RT	0	0	0	0	S	0.0	0.0	0:00.00

13 root ksoftirqd/2	20	0	0	0	0	S	0.0	0.0	0:00.07
14 root watchdog/2	RT	0	0	0	0	S	0.0	0.0	0:06.75
15 root migration/3	RT	0	0	0	0	S	0.0	0.0	0:00.00
16 root stopper/3	RT	0	0	0	0	S	0.0	0.0	0:00.00

We have a number of commands that are like top but need to be installed, such as **htop** and **glances over top**, which needs to be installed if you want to use it.

Kill Utility

Kill is a utility used to stop a command that is running. This utility sends a message called signal to the program or process. We have 64 different signals, some having distinct meanings from stop running:

[ppeters@rad-srv root]$ kill [process ID]

- SIGTERM is the default signal sent by kill and says you want it to stop. It is only a demand, and it can be ignored by the program.

- The SIGKILL signal is absolutely necessary, prompting the process to close immediately. The only exception is for the program to ask the operating system, i.e. a system call, in the middle of it. The fact is that the application must be completed first. The 9th signal is in the list and is normally sent with SIGKILL:

[ppeters@rad-srv root]$ kill -9 [process ID]

- We have a number of ways to tell a command to quit and CTRL-C is the primary method, and this method sends a SIGINT message to the Linux kernel. The second way to cause a process to quit is using the kill command specified with the process ID or PID as an argument to kill.

Uptime

The uptime command or utility in Linux is a tool used basically to show us the amount of time our Linux system has been operational, with load average measurement as well:

[ppeters@rad-srv root]$ uptime

Nice and Renice Utilities

Nice and renice are utilities to alter the process priority in Linux. Finally, you can change processes priority using nice, which runs a process with an altered scheduling priority, while the renice utility changes the priority of running processes.

Linux Environment and Shell Variables

Environment properties or parameters in Linux are system values designated to objects in the operating system that are utilized in the execution of processes. When communicating with your server through the bash shell session, there are a number of pieces of data that your bash evaluates to dictate its conduct and access to Linux system resources. Some of these configurations are embedded in the configuration file and others are ascertained by the user input.

One means the bash shell keeps a record of all these configurations and information is through any location it controls called the Linux environment variable. The Linux environment is a region that the shell creates every time a session opens that comprises variables that classify system attributes.

Environment Set and Env Utilities

In Linux, it is possible to check what environment variables are set for the system using the two commands below. User may get or see the environment parameters and settings in your Linux system by typing the set and env commands as shown below:

[ppeters@rad-srv root]$ set

or
[ppeters@rad-srv root]$ env

Below is the illustration of the env command

 [ppeters@rad-srv ~]$ env

HOSTNAME=rad-srv.uz.ac.zw

SELINUX_ROLE_REQUESTED=

SHELL=/bin/bash

TERM=xterm

HISTSIZE=1000

SSH_CLIENT=10.50.219.53 56324 22

SELINUX_USE_CURRENT_RANGE=

SSH_TTY=/dev/pts/0

USER=ppeters

LS_COLORS=rs=0:di=01;34:ln=01;36:mh=00:pi=40;33:so=01;35:do=01;35:bd=40;33;01:cd=40;33;01:or=40;31;01:mi=01;05;37;41:su=37;41:sg=30;43:ca=30;41:tw=30;42:ow=34;42:st=37;44:ex=01;32:*.tar=01;31:*.tgz=01;31:*.arj=01;31:*.taz=01;31:*.lzh=01;31:*.lzma=01;31:*.tlz=01;31:*.txz=01;31:*.zip=01;31:*.z=01;31:*.Z=01;31:*.dz=01;31:*.gz=01;31:*.lz=01;31:*.xz=01;31:*.bz2=01;31:*.tbz=01;31:*.tbz2=01;31:*.bz=01;31:*.tz=01;31:*.deb=01;31:*.rpm=01;31:*.jar=01;31:*.rar=01;31:*.ace=01;31:*.zoo=01;31:*.cpio=01;31:*.7z=01;31:*.rz=01;31:*.jpg=01;35:*.jpeg=01;35:*.gif=01;35:*.bmp=01;35:*.pbm=01;35:*.pgm=01;35:*.ppm=01;35:*.tga=01;35:*.xbm=01;35:*.xpm=01;35:*.tif=01;35:*.tiff=01;35:*.png=01;35:*.svg=01;35:*.svgz=01;35:*.mng=01;35:*.pcx=01;35:*.mov=01;35:*.mpg=01;35:*.mpeg=01;35:*.m2v=01;35:*.mkv=01;35:*.ogm=01;35:*.mp4=01;35:*.m4v=01;35:*.mp4v=01;35:*.vob=01;35:*.qt=01;35:*.nuv=01;35:*.wmv=01;35:*.asf=01;35:*.rm=01;35:*.rmvb=01;35:*.flc=01;35:*.avi=01;35:*.fli=01;35:*.flv=01;35:*.gl=01;35:*.dl=01;35:*.xcf=01;35:*.xwd=01;35:*.yuv=01;35:*.cgm=01;35:*.emf=01;35:*.axv=01;35:*.anx=01;35:*.ogv=01;35:*.ogx=01;35:*.aac=01;36:*.au=01;36:*.flac=01;36:*.mid=01;36:*.midi=01;36:*.mka=01;36:*.mp3=01;36:*.mpc=01;36:*.ogg=01;36:*.ra=01;36:*.wav=01;36:*.axa=01;36:*.oga=01;36:*.spx=01;36:*.xspf=01;36:

PATH=/usr/local/sbin:/usr/local/bin:/sbin:/bin:/usr/sbin:/usr/bin:/root/bin

MAIL=/var/spool/mail/root

PWD=/home/ppeters

```
LANG=en_US.UTF-8

MODULEPATH=/usr/share/Modules/modulefiles:/etc/modulefiles

LOADEDMODULES=

SELINUX_LEVEL_REQUESTED=

HISTCONTROL=ignoredups

HOME=/home/ppeters

SHLVL=2

LOGNAME=ppeters

CVS_RSH=ssh

SSH_CONNECTION=10.50.219.53 56324 10.17.1.11 22

MODULESHOME=/usr/share/Modules

LESSOPEN=||/usr/bin/lesspipe.sh %s

G_BROKEN_FILENAMES=1

BASH_FUNC_module()=() { eval `/usr/bin/modulecmd bash $*`

}

OLDPWD=/root

_=/bin/env

[ppeters@rad-srv ~]$
```

Export and Echo Utilities in Linux

We can alter the values of an environment variable by using the export and echo commands in Linux:

```
[ppeters@rad-srv root]$ export VAR=<value>
```

- We can check the value using the command below:

```
[ppeters@rad-srv root]$ echo $VAR
```

The Linux environment PATH, also known as the query path, is a catalog of folders under which the Linux shell program is seeking to discover a specific Linux command. For instance, if you enter ls, it will check at /bin/ls. The route is placed in the PATH variable, which is a catalog of folder titles split by the colon and encoded inside./bashrc. You can move or export a fresh path using the command that is below:

```
[ppeters@rad-srv root]$ export PATH=$PATH:/[folder]
```

Bash Variable in Scripts

When we are running a bash shell script, we have pseudo-environment variables which can be called using $1, $2, etc., for the discrete parameters or arguments that were passed to the script when it was run. Furthermore, $0 is the name of the script and the command $@ shows us the list of all the command-line arguments or parameters.

The "~/." Files (dot-files)

The foremost dot in a file in Linux is utilized as a marker to not list these files ordinarily, but only when they are specifically demanded. The motive is that, generally, dot-files are used to store configuration and sensitive data for system programs and applications.

~/.bashrc

- ~/.bashrc this file contains bash scripts and variables that are executed when bash is invoked.

- It is a noble skill and expert knowledge to modify your ~/.bashrc. Linux users should always remember to source their ./bashrc file whenever a modification is made. We should note that opening a fresh Linux shell terminal has a similar outcome as sourcing your file:

[ppeters@rad-srv root]$ source ~/.bashrc

Sensitive Dot-Files

Usage of cryptographic programs, such as ssh and gpg, in Linux keeps a lot of information in the following directories ~/.ssh and ~/.gnupg respectively.

File Descriptors

In Linux, we have filehandles that are also termed file descriptors. File descriptors are unique positive integers that uniquely identify open files in the bash shell. We have three main file descriptors namely 0,1 and 2 that describe how data resources may be accessed. Filehandle 0 refers to data stream STDIN read standard input, whilst filehandle 1 represents data stream STDOUT read standard, and lastly filehandle 2 refers to data stream STDERR read standard error.

The file descriptor designation is used for the management of these Linux system files and resources in the bash shell terminal. As an illustration, to direct a system input to a command, we utilize the less than sign < **as shown below**:

[ppeters@rad-srv root]$ [COMMAND] < [INPUT]

- To send a command's output somewhere other than the terminal screen such as a file on the system or a new one, you use > **greater than sign**. For example, to just discard the output altogether you redirect the command to the /dev/null :

[ppeters@rad-srv root]$ [COMMAND] > /dev/null

- We use fd 02 to direct the program's error messages to a file as demonstrated below:

[ppeters@rad-srv root]$ [COMMAND] 2> [FILE_NAME]

- To direct the Linux command's standard error messages to the identical place where the terminal console's standard output is displayed, i.e. combining it into a single stream through pipelining as shown by the command below:

[ppeters@rad-srv root]$ [COMMAND] 2>&1

Linux File System Permissions

Each file and directory in the Linux Operating System is understood to belong to a specific user who owns or who created the file called the owner, and a specific grouping of users who are part of a group in which the file creator is a member. Files additionally have permissions affirming what tasks are permitted to be done on the file by a user or a group of users.

chmod

A Linux file or directory can take three permissions: read, write, and execute. For a Linux file we have 3 following permissions: read the file, write or edit the file, and to execute or run the file as a program.

For a directory, we have the following permissions: the power to display a listing of the contents of the directory, the ability to create and remove files from inside the directory, and the ability to utilize or manipulate files inside the file system directory. In Linux, we use the chmod utility to alter or modify the file or directory permissions.

chown and chgrp

Standard Linux authorizations do not support access control lists enabling a folder to be exchanged for an intention with a named user list. The administrator should instead place every user in a team and build the file as a part of the user group. Due to the random user list, file owners can't share files. There are three file-related user authorities: user, group, and others. Each of them has an attendant permission like read, write and execute.

We use the chown or change owner command to modify the user who owns the file or folder in Linux.

Linux file systems allow two techniques to configure permissions with the chmod permissions utility:

We have the octal method, which uses three numerical weights for read, write and execute: read is assigned weight of value 4, while write is assigned the weight of value 2, and lastly execute is 1. The total value of permissions is calculated by finding the sum total of the weighted values where each one is found by multiplying user value by 100, group by 10, and lastly others by 1, and sum the values corresponding to the granted permissions.

For instance 766 = 700 + 60 + 6 = rwxrw-rw-:

[ppeters@rad-srv ~]$ chmod 775 [FILE_NAME]

We can also use the abbreviated alphabet-based technique using the following symbols representing user, group and others respectively: **u, g,** or **o.** We use these letters of the alphabet prefixed by either a plus (+) or minus (-) sign, followed by an alphabet letter that represents the permissions, namely r for read, w for write, and x for execute permissions.

The example u+x "gives a user permissions to execute ", g-w, " this illustration takes away write permissions from the group", and o+r, "gives others or the universe read permissions":

[ppeters@rad-srv ~]$ chmod g-w [FILENAME]

We can also modify the group in Linux using the **chgrp** command, by means of the identical logic as the chmod command.

When we want to view the file permissions of every file and directory in the current working folder, we type the statement below:

[ppeters@rad-srv ~]$ ls -l

[ppeters@uofzlbsrv01 etc]$ cd /

[ppeters@uofzlbsrv01 /]$ ls -l

total 16

lrwxrwxrwx. 1 root root 7 Jul 25 10:26 bin -> usr/bin

dr-xr-xr-x. 5 root root 4096 Sep 27 11:26 boot

drwxr-xr-x. 21 root root 3160 Aug 20 16:09 dev

drwxr-xr-x. 77 root root 8192 Sep 27 11:23 etc

```
drwxr-xr-x.  3 root root   21 Jul 25 10:32 home
lrwxrwxrwx.  1 root root    7 Jul 25 10:26 lib -> usr/lib
lrwxrwxrwx.  1 root root    9 Jul 25 10:26 lib64 -> usr/lib64
drwxr-xr-x.  2 root root    6 Apr 11  2018 media
drwxr-xr-x.  2 root root    6 Apr 11  2018 mnt
drwxr-xr-x.  4 root root   44 Jul 30 15:35 opt
dr-xr-xr-x. 283 root root    0 Aug 20 16:08 proc
dr-xr-x---.  5 root root  253 Jul 30 19:47 root
drwxr-xr-x. 24 root root  800 Sep 27 11:26 run
lrwxrwxrwx.  1 root root    8 Jul 25 10:26 sbin -> usr/sbin
drwxr-xr-x.  2 root root    6 Apr 11  2018 srv
dr-xr-xr-x. 13 root root    0 Aug 20 16:08 sys
drwxrwxrwt.  7 root root   93 Sep 27 11:26 tmp
drwxr-xr-x. 13 root root  155 Jul 25 10:26 usr
drwxr-xr-x. 19 root root  267 Jul 25 16:00 var
[ppeters@uofzlbsrv01 /]$
```

Reading from the output of an ls -l command , the result drwxr-xrw- means we have a directory file (d) where the directory owner has read (r) and write (w) and execute permissions, and the group has read and execute but no write permissions and lastly others have reading and writing permissions.

Listing or Searching for Files

Ls command

The ls command lists the contents which can be either files or directories in the current working directory. We have a number of options or switches we can use with the ls command. The most used switch is the -l flag used to display a list of files and directories and their inherent permissions. We also have the option -a flag which displays all the files and directories including the dot-files:

```
[ppeters@rad-srv root]$ ls -la
```

We can also display a listing of the files ranked by size:

```
[ppeters@uofzlbsrv01 /]$ ls -Slr
total 16
dr-xr-xr-x. 13 root root    0 Aug 20 16:08 sys
dr-xr-xr-x. 281 root root    0 Aug 20 16:08 proc
drwxr-xr-x.  2 root root    6 Apr 11  2018 srv
drwxr-xr-x.  2 root root    6 Apr 11  2018 mnt
drwxr-xr-x.  2 root root    6 Apr 11  2018 media
lrwxrwxrwx.  1 root root    7 Jul 25 10:26 lib -> usr/lib
```

```
lrwxrwxrwx. 1 root root   7 Jul 25 10:26 bin -> usr/bin

lrwxrwxrwx. 1 root root   8 Jul 25 10:26 sbin -> usr/sbin

lrwxrwxrwx. 1 root root   9 Jul 25 10:26 lib64 -> usr/lib64

drwxr-xr-x. 3 root root  21 Jul 25 10:32 home

drwxr-xr-x. 4 root root  44 Jul 30 15:35 opt

drwxrwxrwt. 7 root root  93 Sep 27 11:26 tmp

drwxr-xr-x. 13 root root 155 Jul 25 10:26 usr

dr-xr-x---. 5 root root 253 Jul 30 19:47 root

drwxr-xr-x. 19 root root 267 Jul 25 16:00 var

drwxr-xr-x. 24 root root 800 Sep 27 11:26 run

drwxr-xr-x. 21 root root 3160 Aug 20 16:09 dev

dr-xr-xr-x. 5 root root 4096 Sep 27 11:26 boot

drwxr-xr-x. 77 root root 8192 Sep 27 11:23 etc

[ppeters@uofzlbsrv01 /]$
```

We can also display the file names of the 5 most newly changed files ending with the .conf extension as shown below:

```
[ppeters@rad-srv root]$ ls -tr *.conf | tail -5
```

Find

This utility or command is used to search for files in a directory:

```
[ppeters@rad-srv root]$ find <DIRECTORY> -name <FILENAME>
```

which

To search for command binaries in PATH variables:

```
[ppeters@rad-srv root]$ which ls
```

whereis

To search for any file in any of the directories:

```
[ppeters@rad-srv root]$ whereis <FILENAME>
```

locate

This command searches for files by name (using slocate database):

```
[ppeters@rad-srv root]$ locate <FILENAME>
```

In Linux you can test if a file exists:

```
[ppeters@rad-srv root]$ test -f <FILENAME>
```

Creating Files and Directories

mkdir

The mkdir command creates a directory. The most useful flag is -p which creates the entire path of directories in case it does not exist:

```
[ppeters@rad-srv root]$ mkdir -p dir_name
```

cp

In Linux, we can copy files from the directory tree through the use of the cp command. We can use the cp command with the switch -a flag to preserve all the file metadata:

```
[ppeters@rad-srv root]$ cp -a source_file dest_file
```

Intriguingly, shell commands bounded by $() can be executed and the resulting output of the instructions is exchanged for the paragraph and can be used as a part of another command in the terminal and illustrated below:

```
[ppeters@rad-srv root]$ cp $(ls -rt *.conf | tail -5) dest_file
```

pushd and popd

The pushd utility or Linux shell command stores the present running directory in Linux computer storage so it can be restored for use when desired, optionally changing to a new directory:

```
[ppeters@rad-srv root]$ pushd ~/Desktop/
```

The Linux popd utility comes back to the path at the top of the Linux file system folder pile.

ln

In Linux, we can link and connect files with different names with the ln command. We can create both soft and hard links. To create a symbolic (soft) link we use the Linux option -s switch as illustrated below:

```
[ppeters@rad-srv root]$ ln -s target name_of_link
```

dd

dd is a Linux command-line utility used for copying and converting files. dd stands for copy and convert used for disk to disk copies. This command is very useful for creating copies of raw disk space. We can use the dd utility for backup in Linux especially when we are making copies of a whole Master Boot Record as shown below:

```
[ppeters@rad-srv root]$ dd if=/dev/hda of=hda.mbr bs=512 count=1
```

We can also utilize dd to make copies of one disk drive onto an alternative one:

```
[ppeters@rad-srv root]$ dd if=/dev/hda of=/dev/hdb
```

Disk and Network Management Utilities

du

This is the disk usage utility which shows how much disk space is used for each file:

[ppeters@rad-srv root]$ du -ah

We can modify our command to display only the sorted and 15 largest files in the current working directory using the command below:

[ppeters@rad-srv root]$ du -a | sort -rn | head -15

We can also alter the commands and add options which help in displaying all the subdirectories that are occupying a lot of disk space:

[ppeters@rad-srv root]$ du --max-depth=1 | sort -k1 -rn

df

This disk-free utility or command df shows the amount of disk space on the file system. The name, size, how much has been used, how much is accessible, use ratio, and where it is installed are all rows on each file system. Note that values are not added because Unix file systems have protected memory websites that can only be written by the kernel consumer.

[ppeters@rad-srv root]$ df -h

ifconfig

The ifconfig which stands for interface configuration is the networking command used to check and configure your Linux network interface as shown below:

[ppeters@rad-srv root]$ ifconfig

dig

The dig utility is a DNS lookup utility that is related to Nslookup utility in Windows Operating System. The dig utility is used to check whether our DNS server is resolving names

netstat

The Linux netstat utility displays all the network associations, network routing table and network interface statistics. We have a wide number of switches or options to use with netstat which are -t switch for TCP, -u switch for UDP, -l switch for listening, -p switch for program, -n for numeric. The illustration below shows the netstat command with the options:

[ppeters@rad-srv root]$ netstat -tulpn

To connect to Linux server or system we can use telnet. The example below shows the telnet on localhost at port 67:

[ppeters@rad-srv root]$ telnet localhost 67

lsof

The lsof command is used to list open files recollect that everything in Linux is considered a file in Linux:

[ppeters@rad-srv root]$ lsof <STRING>

To see open TCP ports:

```
[ppeters@rad-srv root]$ lsof | grep TCP
```

To see IPv4 port(s):

```
[ppeters@rad-srv root]$ lsof -Pnl +M -i4
```

Logs

In Linux, the regular logging facility can be found at path /var/log. For example:

- /var/log/boot.log contains all the information that is logged when the system boots.
- /var/log/auth.log contains all the system authorization logs.
- /var/log/dmesg this file contains kernel ring buffer logged details.

The file /etc/rsyslog.conf this file controls what goes inside the log files.

The folder /etc/services is a plain ASCII file providing a mapping between friendly textual names for internet services, and their underlying assigned port numbers and protocol types. To check it:

```
[ppeters@rad-srv root]$ cat /etc/services
```

```
[ppeters@rad-srv root]$ grep 110 /etc/services
```

To see what your system is logging:

```
[ppeters@rad-srv root]$ lastlog
```

Chapter Two: Introduction to Hacking

Computer Systems Hacking relates to operations orchestrated to compromise digital devices, such as laptops, smart and digital phones, tablets, and even whole computer networks. Hacking isn't always intended for malicious purposes; today almost all references to hacking and hackers describe it as an unlawful activity by computer hackers who are motivated by monetary gain, political protests, harvesting information illegally through snooping, and so on.

At its core, hacking means changing computer system features to achieve a goal beyond the original purpose of the created IT system. Unendorsed and Unapproved admission to data on an Information Technology system or a computer is the most basic meaning of hacking.

In a methodical, material or individual element, hacking manipulates both system and computer security checks and controls. A hacker is a person who is relentlessly involved in hacking and has accepted hacking as his or her own way of life and viewpoint of their own choosing. Computer hacking is nowadays the most common type of hacking, particularly in cybersecurity. The huge media awareness accorded to black hat hackers is driving the growth of cybercrime and the growth of hacking.

Nevertheless, there are two meanings of the term "hacking." The primary definition refers to the hobbyist computer profession. The ensuing description refers to the alteration or modification of computer hardware or software in a way that alters the system designers' original purpose. It is the art of scheming using computers to gain privileges to access restricted data. Since the world uses IT systems to collect, store and manipulate critical data and information, it is imperative to ensure that the information is safe. However, no system is without is problems. Security systems often contain holes, which allow hackers to access the otherwise limited information if used.

Why Do People Hack?

One of the pointed questions we keep receiving recurrently from users as well as businesses is, why do hackers hack?

When someone attempts to access other people's computer systems in order to damage or alter significant information or data, such activity is described as hacking and the individual who is answerable for this act is called a hacker. Hacking activities are supposedly not based on any logic. Hackers instead try to experiment and show their IT expertise and brilliance by gaining unauthorized access and infecting other computer systems with viruses. Hacking is mainly done to showcase a hacker's incredible Linux, computer systems and programming skills and prove their uncanny abilities to exploit computers to do their bidding. Observing the hacking reasons, we may logically conclude that hacking is done with the major aim of acquiring critical information from IT systems and an inherent desire to disrupt systems through viral infections.

From research and following many hackers, we found out that there are several motives why hackers perform a hack. Hackers hacked websites or took down services in the early days of the internet just to show that they could break a system. So, you might say that it was more about the hacker's ego or showcasing, or sometimes just merely trying to point out that the IT system or service could be broken. It is much more complex these days and so are the motives behind all these hacking activities.

In the following sections we are going to put out the major reasons believed to be behind all hacking activities.

To Steal Information

One of hackers' most common grounds for hacking is stealing personal, or organizational important information. This could be your customer data and information, your internal staff, or even your business-specific private data. These are instances where hackers usually go after large objectives in order to get the most attention.

The Ashley Madison hack or the Starbucks app hack are some of the greatest examples. Hackers entered the Starbucks customer database in the Ashley Madison hack and they had access to all the data including private photos of popular celebrities. This incident has been a major internet shake-up that has also affected many people's private lives.

Hackers often also steal user's personal data to assume their social identity, and then utilize that data for something else, such as money transfers, loans, etc. After internet banking and mobile banking began to become more common, such incidents have risen. The potential for financial profit through hacking has also risen with the development of smartphones and mobile devices.

Many large corporations like Sony, Yahoo, Equifax and eBay have fallen under this hacking trap. Although a lot of media attention has been paid to hacking these companies, most businesses still believe that this will not happen to them.

To Disrupt Services

Hackers just enjoy taking down something and then leaving a statement on the hacked website but, by generating bots that overpower a computer with too many requests as traffic, hackers have effectively taken down many ICT services and infrastructure, leading to a system crash. It is known as the Denial of Service attack commonly termed DoS and can, for a certain time, completely stop the website of a company. DDoS or Distributed Service Denial attacks are also taking place today, using multiple infected systems to download a single major system leading to a denial of service.

There are many other methods, such as infection by email or otherwise of a large network with malicious software, which can lead to a chain reaction affecting the whole network.

Server disruption attacks usually have personal motives of their own. It's primarily about making a service or website ineffective. It could also sometimes be about driving a point home.

Just to Make a Point

Hackers that fit into this group are very exciting. They're not interested in money or data. They appear to have a greater objective in life. They're trying to steal data or interrupt your network to prove a point.

Again, going back to the Ashley Madison hack, the hackers had access to the account information of 32 million customers but before they made this public, the hackers left a message on the website to tell everyone what they were doing. They also stated what they thought about the website and why they believed a service like this was immoral.

Hacking as a Learning Tool

Hacking leads various people to develop new and better software that can dramatically improve the electronic world. Although hacking is a diverse competency, those who hack the longest will succeed because they know how computers work and how they have changed over time. Ethical hackers use their expertise to help improve system, hardware and software vulnerabilities.

The ethical hackers come from a wide range of backgrounds. Ex-nefarious hackers who decide their intentions are to assist in preventing damage to corporations by cracks in their security are the best example. These companies pay their ethical hackers well, as they provide a service that can be good for stopping significant harm and loss.

Single corporations that need advanced protection can employ them while others can be contracted by software designers that will reach millions of people worldwide.

For Financial Gain

This is generally what everybody is afraid of. At the point when they've been compromised and a hacker is demanding cash, we've seen many corporations going out to security experts. Hackers not only infiltrate companies and demand for ransom, but they also attempt to hack into normal user accounts and attempt to take advantage of online banking, internet commerce, and everything that involves financial operations.

In the past few years we saw the largest ransomware assault called WannaCry where millions of devices were hacked around the globe and customers had to deposit a ransom to get back access to their pcs..

For Social Purposes

There is also a particular objective driving many hackers. This comes out every now and then only when they are caught. Some of them strive to be idealists and expose prejudice and injustices in our societies, some have political intentions, some easy public targets. A huge instance is a hacktivist community called Anonymous that has been famous around the globe for questioning many regimes and bringing them down. In order to foster a specific ideology, these hackers can aim for religious communities, regimes and movements.

What is a Hacker?

Hacker is a term used to mean a smart computer programmer, although some imply the term to mean a person who endeavors to hack into computing technology systems. In a more technological view, a hacker is an individual who exploits ICT equipment such as computers, networking equipment and other programming techniques to solve information technology and other technical issues. The word hacker may apply to people who are skilled in technology but often relates to those who use their capability to enter devices and networks unlawful for the purpose of committing offenses or testing the vulnerabilities of the system to help organizations. For example, cybercriminals may steal from people their personal identity, damage or undermine information systems and often hold those platforms hostage for protection money.

Historically, the word "hacker" was divisive and was used sometimes as a word to admire a person with the ability and creativity to tackle technical issues. The word is more frequently used to identify anyone who utilizes this technical ability for unlawful or unethical reasons.

Types of Hackers

Informally, the security community uses hat colors as a manner of identifying distinct kinds of hackers, generally split into three types namely; a white hat, a black hat and a gray hat hacker.

White hat hackers, also recognized as ethical hackers, are trying to work in the greatest interest of the public instead of causing mayhem. Most white hat hackers are doing penetration tests to try to enter into the networks of an organization to identify and disclose security vulnerabilities. The security enterprises assist their clients to alleviate security problems before they can be exploited by criminal hackers.

Intentionally, **Black Hat Hackers** will gain unlawful entry to corporate networks and application systems, either for stealing information, spreading malware, ransomware, vandalizing or even harming computer systems or, for whatever purpose, even just for fame. Black hat hackers are defined as criminals because they breach laws and regulations by accessing systems without permission; they may also participate in several other illicit activities, including identity theft and denial-of-service attacks.

The hackers known as **Gray Hat hackers** are a group of hackers that are between White Hat and Black Hat hackers. Although they may have similar motives to white hat hackers, grey hats are more susceptible to access systems without permission than white hat hackers. At the same time, they are more likely to prevent unnecessary damage to hacker-type systems than black hat hackers. While they aren't typically money-driven, Gray hat hackers can offer to fix their own unauthorized vulnerabilities instead of using their expertise to exploit vulnerabilities for illegal profit.

Hacker vs. Cracker

The term "hacker" was first used in the 1960s for a programmer or individual who could increase the efficiency of the computer code in an age with very limited computer capabilities so that excess computer code instructions were removed or "hackened" from the program. Over the years, it has evolved into a person with advanced computer, networking, programming or hardware skills.

The term "hacker" applies best to many in technology, but over time the term has become used for people who use their skills in a malicious way. The term "scraper" for criminal hackers was proposed for countering the trend of labeling skilled technologists as criminals, with the purpose of removing the stigma from being labeled as a hacker.

Inside the hacker-cracker domain, hackers detect and sort weaknesses in security systems, including security experts, who are tasked with identifying and remedying system faults. On the other hand, crackers are trying to infringe on the computer and network security to take advantage of those same flaws.

Although technologists have promoted using the term cracker over the years, it is common for white hat, gray hat or black hat to be used to distinguish between different-motivated hackers. The term cracker has not found a lot of traction in general use.

What is Cracking?

Cracking is the act of breaching a networked computer system. A cracker may do this, nefariously for financial gain, for a sake alone or a cause, or because there's the challenge.

Cracking does not usually involve a mysterious leap of hacker brilliance, contrary to a widespread myth, but rather perseverance and the stubborn repeat of a few quite famous tricks that exploit common weaknesses in target system safety. Most crackers are therefore just mediocre hackers. These two conditions should not be confused. Hackers typically avoid and hate cracking.

What is Penetration Testing?

In order to improve the defense capability of the systems, penetration tests utilize the tools and techniques of malicious assailants to identify and exploit weaknesses in a system. Tests of penetration require curiosity, intelligence and a willingness to push the boundaries of what is possible.

Penetration Testing, also called pen testing, is a security exercise where an ethical hacker or security expert tries to identify or exploit computer system vulnerabilities. The aim of this simulated attack is to detect any weak points on the defenses of an ICT system that attackers could use.

It's like a bank employing someone as a burglar and attempts to bust in and get entry to the vault. The bank will obtain valuable information as to how to tighten up security measures if it succeeds and enters the bank or the vault.

Who Performs Penetration Tests?

Best of all, someone with little to no prior knowledge of how the system is developed and secured can do a pen test, because they can expose the blind spots that developers that built the system missed. Therefore, the experiments are generally carried out by external consultants. These consultants are often referred to as 'ethical hackers' as they are employed with authorization to access a system with a view to improving security.

Many ethical hackers are sophisticated engineers and certified for pen-testing. Some of the greatest ethical hackers, on the other side, are self-trained. Indeed, some of them are converted hackers who now use their knowledge to solve security weaknesses instead of manipulating them. The best applicant to perform a penetration exam may differ significantly based on the destination business and what sort of pen exam they want to start.

Types of Penetration tests

Black Box Penetration Testing

The hacker will likely not understand the entire ins and outs of a company's IT infrastructure in a true cyber-attack. Therefore, in order to attempt to identify a vulnerability or deficiency, they are latching onto the IT infrastructure by a brute force attack.

In other cases, no details about the inner functioning of the specific system and network infrastructure, nor its source code or software architecture are provided in this sort of penetration test. This specific type of test may therefore take a long time, so that the test tester relies on automated processes to detect the weaknesses and vulnerabilities in a complete measurement. This sort of test is also known as the "trial and error" method.

White Box Penetration Testing

The tester has complete knowledge and access both to the source code and software architectures of the Web Application in this type of pen test, also called "Clear Box Testing." This means that, compared to a Black Box test, a White Box test can be done in a much quicker time frame. The other benefit of this is the ability to carry out a much more detailed pen test.

But there are also many drawbacks to this methodology. First, as a reviewer has a full understanding, it may take longer to decide what to concentrate on system testing and component evaluation. Secondly, more advanced instruments such as software code analyzers and debuggers are needed to carry out this sort of experiment.

Gray Box Penetration Testing

As the title suggests, the black box and the white box test merge this sort of test. In other words, only part of the internal components of the system is known to the penetration tester. Often this is limited to accessing the software code and system architecture diagrams.

Both manual and automated test procedures can be used with the Gray Box Test. This approach allows the pentester to focus their main efforts on those areas that it knows most about and exploit all weaknesses and vulnerabilities, and from there. There is a greater chance that "security holes" can also be found but it is more challenging to locate them using this specific technique.

Covert Penetration Test

This is also referred to as a' double-blind' penetration exam. Nobody in the company knows that the penetration test is taking place, including IT experts and security workers who respond to this attack. For secret checks, in order to prevent issues with law compliance the hacker must have the scope and other test information in advance.

External Penetration Test

The ethical hacker goes against external-facing technology of the organization, such as the company's website and third party network servers, in an external penetration test. It may not even be possible for the hacker to enter the company building in some cases. This can mean attacking from a remote location or testing while you are in a vehicle or car parked nearby.

Internal Penetration Test

An internal test is done by an ethical hacker from the internal network of the company. This type of test is useful to assess how much damage can be caused by an unsound and disgruntled employee from behind the firewall.

Chapter Three: Kali Linux Introduction

Kali Linux is a business-ready, Debian-based Linux security auditing system. Kali Linux is designed for IT System administrators and security specialists to carry out complex penetration screening, forensic assessments, and IT security audits.

Kali Linux has been used by security enthusiasts, professional experts in various areas of IT interest which include system penetration testing, digital forensics, system reverse engineering and vulnerability tests. This culminated from years of ingenuity as well as continuous system development and improvement spanning from Whoppix to Backtrack and to now the Debian GNU/Linux driven complete penetration test framework and the vibrant open-source society all over the world.

It is not a straightforward set of security tools, but rather a versatile framework that professionals, system security practitioners, hackers and learners can use to test their Information technology systems for any vulnerabilities and security loopholes.

Kali Linux's Main Purpose

Although the aim of Kali can rapidly be summed up as penetration assessments and security audits, behind those operations are many distinct jobs. Kali Linux is constructed as a framework, since there are several tools that cover distinct tasks which can definitely be used throughout a penetration test in conjunction with other jobs.

For instance, Kali Linux may be used on multiple kinds of pcs; clearly on the laptop of intrusion testers, but also on servers of system support staff, intending to monitor its network, on workstations of forensic analyzers, etc., in sturdy, embedded devices, usually with ARM CPUs. Many ARM appliances, because of tiny form factors and their low energy demands, are also ideal assault machines. Kali Linux can also be utilized in the cloud in order to rapidly construct a farm of mobile phones and devices to enable really portable penetration testing.

However, that is not all; penetration tests also require servers, to use collaboration software in a team of penetration testers, to set up a Webserver for use in phishing campaigns, to manage tools to scan vulnerabilities and related activities.

Once you start Kali you will soon discover that Kali Linux's main menu is organized thematically across various kinds of tasks and activities, which are relevant for pen testers and other information security professionals.

Kali Linux Users

Kali Linux is genuinely one of the few distinct operating systems that both good and evil men publicly use. White hat, gray hat, black hat hackers and Security Administrators all use this operating system heavily. One for identifying and preventing breaches, and the other for detecting and potentially leveraging these security violations. Kali Linux is the Swiss Army knife in all security tool kits because of the number of tools installed and pre-loaded in the operating system.

Kali Linux Professional Users

1. Systems Security Administrators – These IT professionals are accountable for protecting the information and data of their organizations. You use Kali Linux to check your environment(s) and guarantee that vulnerabilities are not discovered easily and quickly.

2. IT Network Administrators –These professionals are accountable for keeping the network safe and effective. To inspect your network, you use Kali Linux. Kali Linux, for instance, is able to identify rogue dhcp servers and rogue access points within a network..

3. IT Network Architects – These experts Network Architects design protected network settings. They use Kali Linux to check their first renderings and to ensure that they do not overlook or misconfigure anything..

4. Security Penetration Testers – These experts and IT enthusiasts use Kali Linux for auditing IT system environments and gather information and gain an understanding of business environments they are employed to check..

5. Chief Information Security Officers - These use Kali Linux to inspect their workplace internally and to find out if the latest applications or programs or bad configurations have been implemented.

6. Digital Forensic Engineers – Kali Linux has a ' Forensic Mode ' allowing a Forensic Engineer in some cases to discover and recover information.

7. White Hat Hackers – Kali Linux is used by those skilled excellent hackers like Penetration Testers to audit vulnerabilities in a system setting and to find them.

8. Black Hat Hackers – These expert computer hackers use Kali Linux to identify and exploit security flaws. Kali Linux also has countless social engineering apps that a Black Hat Hacker can use to affect an organization or person.

9. Grey Hat Hackers – Lying between White Hat and Black Hat Hackers. They are going to use Kali Linux in the same techniques as the above two

Kali Linux Utilities

For the hacker, Kali Linux Security Distribution is composed of well over 600 pre-loaded penetration testing tools and utilities for use. Each of the pre-loaded application tools comes with its distinctive adaptability and use case. Kali Linux separates all these unique and well-developed utilities into the categories detailed below:

- Information Gathering
- Vulnerability Analysis
- Wireless Attacks
- Web Applications
- Exploitation Tools
- Stress Testing
- Forensics Tools
- Sniffing & Spoofing
- Password Attacks
- Maintaining Access
- Reverse Engineering
- Reporting Tools
- Hardware Hacking

This section of the book is a run-down of these Kali Linux utility categories and what they are endeavoring to achieve.

Information Collection

Information gathering is one of the most eminent and critical steps in successful hacking. Any effective penetration test, security audit and vulnerability assessment are based on strong knowledge and information about your target. If you fail to collect data properly, you may end up targeting random devices that are not susceptible to your attacks. Data collection about a targeted local or global network and its structure, computer identification, its operating systems and the services that operate on the machine are very critical. Identification of possibly delicate information system components. Any experienced hacker has to gather information using a plethora of tools to understand their target better.

Vulnerability Analysis

Quickly testing whether there are aa array of known susceptibilities or unsafe configurations that affect a local or remote machine. The vulnerability detector uses records with thousands of specimens to acknowledge potential vulnerabilities.

Web Application Analysis

Identifying flaws in internet application configurations and security. Identifying and mitigating these problems is essential considering that these apps' public accessibility makes them suitable aims for attackers.

Database Assessment

Database attacks are a very popular vector for attackers from SQL injection to attacking authorizations. Here you can find tools for testing attack vectors from SQL injection to information extraction and assessment.

Password Attacks

Authentication schemes are always a vector for attack. You can find many helpful tools here, from internet password search tools to offline attacks against encoding or hashing schemes.

Wireless Attacks

The widespread existence of wireless networks implies that they will always be a frequently attacked vector. With its broad spectrum of support for various cable devices, Kali is a clear option for attacks against various kinds of wireless networks.

Reverse Engineering

Reverse engineering is a multi-purpose undertaking. In the assistance of offensive tasks, it is one of the main techniques of vulnerability detection and exploitation. On the protective hand, the malware used in directed assaults is analyzed. In this ability, the objective is to define the capacities of a specified item of craft.

Exploitation Tools

Using a (formerly recognized) weakness or getting benefit from it enables you to obtain power over a distant machine (or apparatus). This entry can then be used for additional utility escalation assaults, either locally on the affected computer or on other available computers on its local network. This range includes a range of instruments and instruments that simplify the writing process for your own achievements.

Sniffing & Spoofing

It is often advantageous for an intruder to gain entry to the information system as they move across the computer network. Here you can discover spoofing methods for impersonating a lawful person as well as sniffing systems for capturing and analyzing information directly from the wire. These instruments can be very strong when used together.

Post Exploitation

When you have access to the computer system, you will often want to keep that level of admission or extend authority by going laterally across the network. Tools that help to achieve these objectives can be discovered here.

Digital Forensics

Forensic Linux virtual boot settings have been very common for years. Kali includes a large number of common Linux-based forensic tools that allow you to do everything from original triage, information processing, complete assessment and problem management.

Reporting Tools

Only after the results have been recorded is a penetration test finished. This classification includes tools to assist collect if information from data gathering tools, find non-obvious interactions and put everything together in different reports.

Social Engineering Tools

The chance of exploiting human behavior as an attack vector often occurs when the technical part is well-secured. Because of the correct impact, it is often possible to induce individuals to carry activities that sacrifice environmental safety. Has there been a benign PDF in the USB key that the clerk just plugged in? Or was it a Trojan horse that set up a backdoor as well? Was the accountant's banking page just entered into the database anticipated or a good duplicate used for phishing reasons? This classification includes instruments to help with these kinds of assaults.

System Services

This Kali Linux class comprises of the tools that permit you to start and stop system services that are just Linux programs running in the system background.

Main Kali Linux Features

This Linux hacking distribution comprises a built-in assortment of around 400 application system tools purposely custom-made for targeted grouping of users who may be systems administrators, Linux security experts, penetration testers and many other ICT Professionals.

Kali Linux is abundant with features that distinguish this hacking distribution from other common Linux distributions like Red Hat and Suse Linux. Most of Kali Linux features are bespoke to cater to the particular needs of penetration testers and ICT security experts. The ensuing sections below detail the various qualities.

Kali Linux Live Mode

Differing from most Linux OS flavors, Kali Linux's downloadable ISO image is not purely devoted OS installations on the hardware infrastructure; but can be used as a bootable live system. This evidently means that users can work with Kali Linux without having to install it. Users just need to boot available Live System ISO image which can be written to a USB disk or burnt onto a DVD.

The Kali Linux live mode has the penetration testing, vulnerability assessment and information gathering or reconnaissance tools most frequently used by all types of hackers. In the Live Mode you just basically insert your DVD or USB disk and restart your machine to run Kali. Please note that the default Live Kali Linux Mode does not preserve any modifications between reboots. It is possible to persist any changes made in Kali Live System by configuring persistence with a USB and the changes will be remembered through system restarts.

Kali Linux Forensic Mode

Kali Linux distribution comes preconfigured with the Forensics mode. Typically when conducting digital forensic tasks on a computer system, you need to avoid activities that may modify the records on the system being assessed. Enabling the Forensic mode disables all automounts and activities that may change the system being analyzed.

The Kali Linux live mode is specifically beneficial for digital forensics aims, since it is feasible to reboot any PC into a Kali OS without opening or altering its hard drives and file system.

Bespoke Kernel

Kali Linux permanently delivers a tailored and current Debian Unstable based Linux kernel. This guarantees concrete hardware support, mainly for an extensive array of wireless devices. This bespoke Linux kernel is patched for wireless injection support which is a feature required by wireless security analysis tools.

Kali Linux installs the latest firmware files required by hardware devices typically found in the /lib/firmware/ directory, incorporating the firmware available in Debian's non-free section.

Entirely Customizable

Kali Linux is a tailor-made distribution. It is developed by penetration testers to be used by penetration testers. The developers of Kali Linux have ensured that it is easy to adapt and modify the System based on user requirements and likings. The Kali Linux live-build configuration which is normally used to build the official Kali images is published publicly to enable users to mold Kali Linux to their requirement. Users can easily start from this published live-build configuration and apply several alterations based on their desires, acknowledging the adaptability of the Kali Linux live-build.

Kali Linux live-build incorporates countless features to alter the installed system, install additional files, bonus packages, run random instructions, and change the values pre-seeded to debconf.

A Trustworthy Distribution

It is of the utmost importance for Linux security distributions to be able to be trusted and be depended upon. Kali Linux is developed by a community of developers who are working collaboratively and have availed the distribution's source code, permitting everyone to examine the source code. Kali Linux is developed following the best security practices such as uploading authorized source packages, which are subsequently built on dedicated build daemons. The packages are then check-summed and distributed as part of a signed repository.

The job prepared on the packages can be completely evaluated within the Git repositories which include signed tags used to make the Kali Linux source packages. The progression of every package can be tracked using the Kali Linux package tracker.

Kali on ARM Devices

The Kali Linux operating system and its tools are useable on many system architectures such as the ARM architecture. This operating system offers some binary bundles for use on armel, armhf, and arm64 ARM system architectures. Kali Linux can be implemented on several fascinating devices, ranging from smart watches to smart devices like tablets and to assorted computers.

Security Policies on Kali Linux

Although Kali Linux attempts to shadow the Debian Linux policy when feasible, the developers of Kali Linux have knowingly followed distinctive implementation options due to the different and specific needs of IT security experts.

Specific Kali Linux Root

The many Linux distributions recommend the usage of a non-privileged user account whilst operating the Linux system and the use of sudo utility for user escalation of privileges when required. This security policy, especially in Debian Linux, provides an additional tier of security between the user and several hypothetically dangerous or damaging Linux commands or operations.

Kali Linux security tools are only executed by users with root privileges. The root user is the default Kali user account. During the installation of Kali Linux, the systems administrator will not be urged to make or add a non-privileged user. Learners should be particularly vigilant when using Kali Linux as most damaging errors occur when functioning with root privileges.

Disabled Network Services

Kali Linux, by default, deactivates several installed Linux network and system services that would watch on a public network interface, such as HTTP and SSH. The reasoning following this resolution is to reduce contact during a penetration test when it is disadvantageous to publicize your presence and aid discovery. It is still possible to manually enable any services of your choice through executing the systemctl enable *service*.

Curated Application Programs

Since Debian aims to be the worldwide operating system of choice they make no restrictions on what gets maintained in packages.

Contrastingly Kali Linux only packages the elite freely available penetration testing tools.

Kali Linux developers who are doubling up as penetration testers are the main drivers of the application tools' selection process. The selection process leverages their experience and skill to make the best selections. Kali Linux ensures that we maintain a modernized and valuable penetration testing tool depository. Kali welcomes tool suggestions in a devoted class through the *New Tool Requests* found in the Kali Bug Tracker. All new application utility appeals are accepted better when Kali receives well-presented submissions, comprising a justification of why the tool is valuable, and detail of how it competes with other similar tools.

Summary

This chapter was an introduction to the security and hacking distribution called Kali Linux, we ran through the distribution's major features, with a presentation of numerous usage instances. We discussed some of Kali Linux's adopted policies during the development of Kali Linux.

This Linux variant is a corporate-ready security assessment, penetration testing and IT system auditing Linux distribution grounded on Debian Linux. Kali Linux is targeted at security professionals, IT administrators and other IT professionals permitting them to execute advanced penetration testing, digital forensic investigation, and IT security audits.

Kali Linux is a developing Linux distribution, which describes the fact that there is continuous improvement of the distro *where we receive system updates on a daily basis*. The Kali Linux operating system is a Debian testing-based security distribution. Subsequently, all the security and hacking packages in Kali Linux all come from the Debian Testing package depository.

Though Kali's main focus can be narrowly outlined as network penetration testing and safety auditing, there are various usage cases involving network surveillance, electronic forensic investigation and wireless network monitoring to list only a few.

The Kali Linux security operating system has a range of advanced features that include a live system usage mode, an agile and harmless Kali forensic mode, Linux-based kernel, complete system adaptability, a stable and safe basic operating framework, ARM configuration expertise, secure network policy, and a controlled and tracked user team.

Live Mode Kali Linux

Kali Linux simplifies the process of getting started, because they have *live ISO images*, implying that you can boot and start accessing the Kali Linux environment without any prior installation process. It is possible to use the Kali Linux ISO image as a testing platform, usage as USB/DVD-ROM images in digital forensics cases, and lastly for permanent installation on physical or virtual platforms.

Kali Linux is often the OS of choice for most people with hostile goals, whether they are government-funded groups, parts of structured crime, or individual hackers. Kali Linux simplifies the process of building and distributing bogus versions because of its open-source nature. It is fundamental that you ensure that you download your Kali Linux Live and installation DVDs from authentic sources. It is also critical to always verify the integrity and authenticity of your download through the available means. This is particularly pertinent to ICT security specialists and system administrators who regularly have access to sensitive setups and are trusted with customer records and information.

Where to Find Kali 2019.3 Download

At the time of this book writing, the latest version of Kali Linux is Kali Linux 2019.3 version. The single authorized and authentic source of Kali Linux ISO images is Kali Linux main website's Downloads section. Kali Linux is very popular hence there may be numerous websites offering Live and Kali ISO Image downloads; most of these sources should not be considered as dependable since they may be infected with malware. The link below is the sole authentic and dependable source for Kali Linux downloads.

https://www.kali.org/downloads/

The domain www.kali.org is an SSL platform utilizing electronic encryption certificates. This website is supported by the TLS / SSL Transfer Protocol to HyperText which makes it harder to imitate. A man-in-the-middle attack is not sufficient because the culpable will need a credential www.kali.org certified by the certificate authority Transportation Layer Security (TLS), which is licensed by the victims ' user.

While certificate bodies strive specifically to prevent this type of issue, they also give certificate credentials for candidates who have verified their identity and who have given credential proof that they are the owners of the website. The official download page shows a comprehensive list of ISO images, both 32-bit and 64-bit images used on most contemporary machines and notebooks. You already have a 64-bit processor when you install it for use on a fairly modern computer. When you don't know the processor size, be assured that 32-bit instructions run or execute in all 64-bit processors. Users can download and run the 32-bit images anytime since they run on either 64-bit or 32-bit processors. The opposite does not apply, nevertheless.

If a user is forecasting installing Kali on embedded devices such as smartwatches, smartphones, Chromebooks and wireless access points, or any other piece of equipment that has ARM processors, download Linux *armel* or *armhf* images from the list shown below.

Image Name	Torrent	Version	Size	SHA256Sum
Kali Linux 32-Bit	Torrent	**2019.3**	2.9G	3fdf8732df5f2e935e3f21be93565a113be14b4a8eb410522df60e1c4881b9a0
Kali Linux 64-Bit	Torrent	**2019.3**	2.9G	d9bc23ad1ed2af7f0170dc6d15aec58be2f1a0a5be6751ce067654b753ef7020
Kali Linux Large 64-Bit	Torrent	**2019.3**	3.5G	dd44391927d38d91cae96ed1a8b918767d38bee2617761fab2d54ad8c77319ec
Kali Linux Light ARMhf	Torrent	**2019.3**	803M	9cee49c35400af04e127537a090b9b31b2440cac8cd2568bcaeeb6f4eb4e5a9d
Kali Linux Light 64-Bit	Torrent	**2019.3**	1.1G	b6e57c2d9a22cf73ead39d9d58033991bdaa4769c74e1a9d7174e574d1618af8
Kali Linux Light 32-Bit	Torrent	**2019.3**	1.1G	086c017dbfdf034b6c1114de1be5d3decd6e632cacd63d5d9be2a99c736e9933

			2.7G	44de78249f4b2d4adedc5b40c134933f9b891414dbd54f7fa1d74c99d25dc2a7
Kali Linux LXDE 64-Bit	Torrent	**2019.3**		
Kali Linux MATE 64-Bit	Torrent	**2019.3**	2.8G	8911f11fc8aef74adcfc216e026f431d456237d14bc519c291580103a75750cd
Kali Linux E17 64-Bit	Torrent	**2019.3**	2.7G	f3d37e3dc7c0d66dec04e4d7c636a91139352d6575f7f8a05837e123a4c7af78
Kali Linux KDE 64-Bit	Torrent	**2019.3**	3.2G	7711e0ddd2247c2e50bdb182a9501dd4f775951ab0e84b68f37b689289931576
Kali Linux XFCE 64-Bit	Torrent	**2019.3**	2.7G	c169f63cdb3f5568d111f536d6afd70b635808a614de23a4b2c49073f059f156
Kali Linux 64-bit VMware	Available on the Offensive Security VM Download Page			
Kali Linux 32-bit (PAE) VMware	Available on the Offensive Security VM Download Page			
Kali Linux 64-bit VirtualBox	Available on the Offensive Security VM Download Page			
Kali Linux 32-bit (PAE) VirtualBox	Available on the Offensive Security VM Download Page			

32-bit or 64-bit image?

For any Linux operating system, we have to determine whether we are going to install a 32-bit or 64-bit version of the OS. To make this determination we can examine the flags field in the /proc/cpuinfo virtual text file. The flags are used to determine if the processor is 32-bit and 64-bit. If the flag has the **lm** attribute, then you know your CPU is a 64-bit; otherwise, it is a 32-bit. The ensuing command line will tell you what kind of CPU you have:

```
grep -qP '^flags\s*:.*\blm\b' /proc/cpuinfo && echo 32-bit || echo 64-bit
```

The default Kali Linux and the Kali Linux Light variants are live ISOs that can either run in a live environment and can also be downloaded and set up physically on the machine. These are only distinct because of the pre-installed software packages. The standard Kali Linux ISO image includes the GNOME environment and a large selection of software bundles specifically reserved for most Penetration Testers, and an XFCE-interface that requires significantly fewer system resources and a small percentage of features to pick only the programs you need.

When your selected Kali Linux ISO image is being downloaded you should note down the checksum in the sha256 column of the Kali Linux download page.

Kali ISO Image Authentication

Information Technology Security experts should maintain the reliability of their software to safeguard their data and defend their networks, including those of their customers. Although SSL certificates secure the Kali Linux login site, the actual upload website link leads to an unencrypted URL without protection and that has a potential man-in-the-middle attack. The Kali Linux OS relies heavily on external mirror networks that share downloaded files, so our confidence in these mirror networks should not be blind. There is a high chance that the mirror to which you were led has been hacked, and that you may be the target of an intrusion yourself.

The Kali Linux project continuously provides iso image checksums to mitigate attacks. It is important to always confirm that the checksum you have is issued by the Kali Linux project in order to carry out active checks. We have a number of ways to assess it.

Virtual Kali Linux

Virtual machines have a wide number of advantages for Kali Linux professionals. Virtual machines are essentially helpful when you just want to have a feel of Kali Linux, but are not keen to commit to have a permanent installation of Kali Linux on your physical hardware infrastructure. Virtual machines may also be helpful when you have a powerful server infrastructure that you would like to leverage and use effectively to concurrently run a multitude of operating systems. Virtual machines, especially Oracle VirtualBox, are a great choice for numerous penetration testers and IT security professionals who may still desire total access to their main operating system, whilst they are using Kali Linux hacking and vulnerability assessment tools. It is helpful as well since the expert may just delete the instance of a virtual machine without necessarily reinstalling their whole operating system.

Most virtual environments offer a snapshot feature which makes it incredibly easy and safe to experiment with possibly hazardous procedures, such as malware analysis. The Kali Linux user running Kali on virtual machines is able to just restore to a previous snapshot if their virtual instance is damaged through Kali assessments or usage of malware to test.

We have a variety of virtualization technologies for the PC that are available for all major operating systems like Windows, MacOSX and Linux, namely Oracle *VirtualBox, VMware Workstation for Windows, VMware Fusion for MacOSX, Xen, KVM,* and *Hyper-V* to name a few. Eventually, people choose the virtualization tool that suits their environment and their tastes. In this book we are going to use Oracle VirtualBox on MacOSX and VMware on Windows. These tools are the most frequently used in virtualization desktop software. If there are no business policy restraints or restrictions or any personal preferences, we recommend that the learner try out Oracle VirtualBox, as it is a freely available solution, which works pretty well, is very much open-source, and is useable on most operating systems.

Kali Installation Steps

Initially to begin your installation, you need to boot with your preferred installation medium. When you are using Kali Linux ISO images on your Virtualization host machine, you select the iso image in your installation source prompt. After starting the virtual machine, you are greeted with the Kali Boot screen. `The learner should choose either *Graphical* or *Text-Mode* install. In this illustration, we selected a Graphical Install to initiate installation in graphical mode. If you are comfortable with Text-based installation, you may choose that as an alternative. If you desire to just have a test run of the kali environment without fully installing it, you may select the Live Mode and test out Kali.

After starting the installation process, the user is taken to a screen that prompts them to select a language of choice and then choose your country. The installer is also be prompted to set their keyboard. Users are also expected to specify their geographic location.

The Kali Linux installer will make a copy of the Linux image on your hard drive, and it will then probe your NICs or network interface cards, and then prompt you to enter your system hostname.

You may optionally specify your default domain name for your Kali Linux system to use.

Next up, you need to specify a full name for a non-root user for the system. A primary user ID will be set up, centered on the full name you entered above. Users may change this if they so desire.

Next, set your time zone. And you're all set.

Chapter Four: Basic Networking Concepts

The first stage in building a fully functional system for use during our hacking lessons is to download and install the Kali Linux 2019.3 distribution. Just about all machines are now connected to other computers through networks. It is important for the novice hacker to get acquainted with Linux servers, and gain a good grasp of networking knowledge and the issues related to networking Linux machines.

The initial networking chapter forms the basis for building the subsequent Linux networking, configuration and troubleshooting sections. Those sections will then address the remaining topics discussing Linux network services, the generic network deployment and configuration.

Understanding the Networking topics presented here is going to help in answering the various questions posed to the hacker or novice Linux professional sometimes every day. This will contribute to making the path to Kali Linux less difficult, which begins with an understanding of the OSI and TCP / IP network frameworks.

OSI Reference Model

Developed by the International Organization for Standardization, the Open System Interconnection (OSI) network reference model describes how different hardware and software system components exchanging data should interact and communicate.

In the OSI framework, the level of responsibility is delegated to each element in the data communication route, a realm that it governs and controls. Every layer extracts the authorization, or header details it requires from the data or payload, and uses it to properly transfer the data or information left to the next layer. This layer often removes its authorization and passes the information to the next stage, so that the process is seven layers long.

The first layer of the OSI reference framework specifies the communication attributes of wireless and cable signals used for each "connection" or phase along the route. The second layer or Layer 2 defines the techniques to be used for error correction on the interface. The third layer or Layer 3 guarantees that the data is able to hop from link-to-link on their path to the destination as detailed in their headers. When the information finally arrives, the fourth layer or layer 4 header will be used to decide which locally configured software application will receive it. The application uses Layer 5 rules to monitor the different communication sessions with remote computers and uses Layer 6 to make sure the messages or the file format is right. Layer 7 eventually determines what the end-user will see in the form of a user interface, whether it is a graphic user interface on a monitor or a command-line interface. The table below is an explanation of the purpose of each of the seven OSI layers.

The Seven OSI Layers

Layer #	Layer Name	Explanation	Ports
7	Application	The network application and end-user process interaction layer	NFS Telnet HTTP FTP Sendmail SNMP RPC
6	Presentation	Translates, compresses and encrypts data from one presentation data format to the other.	
5	Session	Establishes, manages and terminates communication sessions between computers and applications	
4	Transport	Manages the formation and destroying of connections. It ensures reliable message delivery especially with TCP. Guarantees that anonymous data is retransmitted. Accurately re-orders data packets that arrive in the wrong order. The protocol data unit in Layer 4 is called a **segment**.	TCP SPX UDP
3	Network	Takes care of the forwarding and transmission of data or packets from one network to the next amongst connections not actually linked together. Data in Layer 3 is called a **packet**.	IP ARP
2	Link	The layer is responsible for Error control and error-free transfer of data frames. Data is called a **frame in Layer 2**.	PPP FDDI ARP
1	Physical	Denotes the electrical and optical signals that go through the medium and interfacing hardware	Ethernet ATM RS232

TCP/IP Introduction

TCP / IP is a standard universal set of protocols used for network connectivity. It belongs to the bigger OSI reference model on which the majority of data communications is based on.

The Internet Protocol (IP) is a component of TCP / IP that guarantees the information is transferred from one address to the next without interference.

For management purposes, the information typically is separated into several bits or packets, each with its own error detection bytes in the packet header or control portion. Upon collecting the packets, the remote computer reconstructs the information and searches for errors. The information is then sent to the system that intends to obtain it.

How is the machine informed of which system requires the information? In its header, the type-field, each IP packet provides a piece of information. It advises the device that is obtaining information on the transport mechanism of layer 4.

Transmission Control Protocol (TCP) and User Datagram Protocol (UDP) are the two most common communication frameworks used on the Internet.

Upon specifying the form of transport protocol, the TCP / UDP header is examined for the port property that is used to identify the network service or application on the device is meant to process the request..

The TCP Protocol

In order to enable many intermittent streams of data to be transmitted over an infinite period of time, TCP opens up a virtual connection between client and server programs operating on individual computers. TCP ensures the monitoring of the received packets by providing each a sequence number with the remote server sending the appropriate delivery confirmation packets. TCP-using applications therefore have a way to discover communication errors and demand the lost packets be retransmitted. TCP is an excellent example of a protocol based upon a connection.

TCP Connection-Oriented Protocol

For communication to become effective, every form requires some kind of acknowledgment. Someone knocks at the gate of a building, the individual inside says, "Who is it?" and the intruder responds, "It's me!" and the door opens. They already realized who was on the other side of the door before it unlocked, and now a dialogue should begin.

Any kind of communication requires a kind of validation to make it meaningful.

TCP works like that. When two devices are communicating, they acknowledge each other. The connection initiator server sends a segment in the TCP header with the SYN bit. The target device for the communication responds with a segment that has its SYN and ACK bits set, to which the initiating server responds with the ACK bit set segment. This communication process with SYN, SYN-ACK, and ACK procedure is commonly known as the "three-way handshake".

The interaction progresses with a sequence of section swaps, each with the ACK bit array. When one of the servers has to stop the interaction, it sends a segment to the other with the FIN and ACK bits set, to which the other client always responds with the FIN-ACK segment The conversation stops with the final ACK from the server that decided to terminate the session.

Below we have the capture of a three-way handshake. You can plainly perceive the three-way handshake to link and disconnect the session.

```
server1 -> server2 TCP 1443 > http [SYN]       Seq=866 Ack=0 Win=5840 Len=0

server2 -> server1 TCP http > 1443 [SYN,ACK] Seq=8404 Ack=867 Win=5792 Len=0

server1 -> server2 TCP 1443 > http [ACK]       Seq=867 Ack=8405 Win=5840 Len=0

server1 -> server2 HTTP HEAD/HTTP/1.1

server2 -> server1 TCP http > 1443 [ACK]       Seq=8405 Ack=1185 Win=54 Len=0

server2 -> server1 HTTP HTTP/1.1 200 OK

server1 -> server2 TCP 1443 > http [ACK]       Seq=1185 Ack=8672 Win=6432 Len=0

server2 -> server1 TCP http > 1443 [FIN, ACK] Seq=8672 Ack=1185 Win=54 Len=0

server1 -> server2 TCP 1443 > http [FIN, ACK] Seq=1185 Ack=8673 Win=6432 Len=0

server2 -> server1 TCP http > 1443 [ACK] Seq=8673 Ack=1186 Win=54
```

The trace above shows that the sequence number denotes the sequential or serial number of the initial byte of information in the segment. The opening line details that an indiscriminate value of 866 was allocated to the foremost byte and all successive bytes for the connection from this server will be serially tracked. This makes the subsequent byte in segment number 867, the third sequence number 868 and so on. The segment acknowledgment number or Ack, not the same as the **ACK** bit, is the byte sequential number of the next segment it anticipates to get from the other end, and the aggregate amount of bytes cannot surpass the **Win** or **window value** that follows it. If the content is not processed accurately, the recipient must re-send the initiating segment calling for the details to be transmitted again. The TCP protocol keeps a record of all this, as well as the source and destination ports including IP addresses, to ensure that each special link is properly serviced.

Connection-less UDP Protocol

User Datagram Protocol, also known as UDP, is a networking protocol that works without establishing a connection between the conversing devices. It is a connection-less protocol. Content or a datagram is transmitted on a "best effort basis with the device which receives the data without any way to check that the remote computer processed the data correctly. UDP is typically used for systems where the data submitted is not project-critical. It has also been used when information has to be sent to all accessible databases on a locally connected network where the formation of hundreds of TCP links for a brief data burst is known to be resource-hungry.

TCP and UDP Ports

The IP packet's data section comprises a segment put within TCP or UDP. Sequence information is contained only in the TCP section header, but the UDP and TCP segment headers monitor the port being used. The client and server's source and destination port, source/destination IP addresses are then merged to classify each data flow individually..

Different globally recognized ports are dedicated to certain services. Port 80 which is HyperText Transfer Protocol is reserved for Web traffic, and port 25 is reserved for Simple Mail Transfer Protocol messages. To system functions proprietary ports below 1024 are allocated, and for third-party program ports that are above 1024 are usually reserved..

Normally, when linking a network-wide device requesting information to a server storing the data, the user chooses a random "origin" port that is currently unused above 1024 and queries the server on the application-specific "destination" port. The database accepts a network port 80 as an HTTP request and passes on the information to be managed by the code of the webserver if this is an HTTP request, the user will use a reference Port 2049 or port 80 (HTTP) as a request. The TCP request will be directed back to port 2049 of the network using the web reference port 80 if the Web server code addresses the question.

The user records all its queries to the IP address of the server and knows the response on port 2049 is not "NFS" initialization, but a response to the original HTTP port 80 application.

The TCP/IP "Time to Live" Feature

Every IP packet has a Time to Live portion (TTL) which records the number of network devices that the packet is moving across to its destination The server which transfers the packet sets the original TTL value, and each network computer that moves the packet decreases the value by 1. The network machine discards the packet if the TTL value hits0.

This method helps to ensure that poor internet routing will not allow packets to go on continuously without leaving the network. Thus, TTLs help to reduce the congestion of the network caused by unwanted traffic data that loops.

TCP/IP's and ICMP Protocol

The Internet Control Message Protocol (ICMP) is another widely used protocol. This protocol is not an exclusively TCP / IP protocol, however other TCP / IP-based applications often use it.

ICMP offers a set of fault control and data alerts for use by the operating system. For instance, sometimes IP packets may arrive on a server with compromised data due to a number of causes including a bad connection; electromagnetic disturbance, or even misconfiguration. Normally this is detected by the server by inspecting the packet and comparing the contents with what it detects in the error management portion of the IP header. It will then give the initial receiving device an ICMP reject message saying that the information should be re-sent because the original transfer was damaged.

ICMP also provides echo or echo reply messages to validate network connectivity using the Linux ping command. When the TTL in a packet is reduced to zero, ICMP TTL expired messages are also transmitted back to the source server by network equipment.

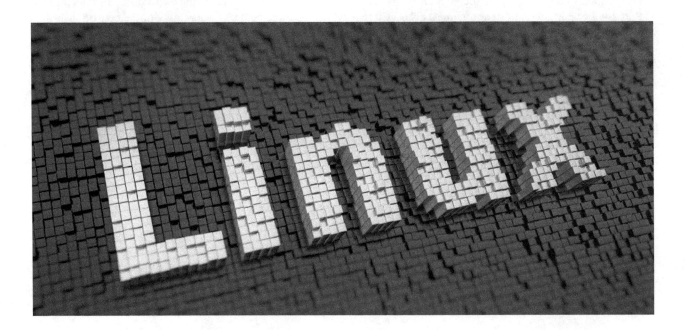

IP Addressing

All Internet-connected devices allowed by TCP / IP have an Internet Protocol (IP) address. Like a phone number, this helps to identify a device user uniquely. The IANA is liable for distributing IP addresses to Internet Service Providers, determining the addresses to use for the public Internet and which IP addresses to use on the private networks.

In fact, IP addresses are a sequence of 32 binary numbers or bits. Network engineers also split these 32 bits into four 8-bit (or byte) sets each reflecting a number from 0 to 255 for ease of use. Then each number is split by a period or dot (.) to construct the usual dotted-decimal notation. 172.16.34.54 is an example of dotted decimal notation.

Private IP Addresses

We have three ranges of IP addresses that were and are reserved for usage merely in private networks and are not publicly forwarded and routed over the Internetwork. We call these **private IP addresses** and below is the 3 ranges:

Class A:	10.0.0.0 - 10.255.255.255
Class B:	172.16.0.0 - 172.31.255.255
Class C:	192.168.0.0 - 192.168.255.255

The pertinent question is, how do all devices configured with private Internet Protocol addresses access the Internet? We will cove how this is done in the NAT section of the book.

Loopback IP Address

All computers, whether or not they have network interface cards, have an in-built loopback Internet Protocol address used by all network-aware applications on the computer to interconnect with one another. Loopback or localhost IP addresses are written commonly as 127.0.0.1.

NAT - Network Address Translation

The inter-network gateway which can be either a router or a firewall is configured to make it look like that all devices such as your laptops and servers on your network have a **publicly routable IP address**, and not a "private" IP address. The concept of using the public IP address on the router or firewall by all machines which are only configured with private IP addresses is called **network address translation or abbreviated NAT** or **IP masquerading** in the Linux world. There exist numerous noble intentions for this, the two most generally specified are:

- People on the public internet do not know the true IP address of the machine as it is behind the router and is using the router's IP Address to access the internet. NAT guards your PCs by allocating them either Class A, B or C private IP addresses that are not transmitted over the Internet. This foils hackers from straightforwardly attacking your Local Area Machines and systems because packets sent to the private LAN IP address will certainly not pass over the Internet.

- We can have a multitude of PCs and IT equipment behind a NAT device masquerading as a single public IP address that belongs to the NAT device. This significantly upturns the total number of devices that can access the Internet without needing extra Public IP version 4 addresses that are running out.

On Linux servers, we can configure Network Address Translation to be **one to one,** where we make a request to our ISP to allocate us a number of public IP addresses to be utilized by the Public internet facing interface of your firewall or router. You then couple each of these public IP addresses to a matching server on your secure private IP network. We are also able to configure a **many to one** Network Address Translation, in which the firewall or gateway maps just a specific IP address to several servers on your local area network.

As a typical regulation, you are not able to access the publicly routable NAT IP addresses from servers on your local or campus network. Elementary Network Address Translation assessment demands someone outside your network to try to connect to your internal network from the Internet.

NAT Port Forwarding

In a modest local area or campus network, all Linux networking servers accessing the Internet seem to show that they are using one specific public IP address of the Internet gateway because of many to one Network Address Translation. Routers and or firewalls can easily keep track of all the various outbound connections to the Internet by monitoring the traffic since they are the gateway to the Internet. The IP addresses and the TCP ports use by each server are mapped to those of the internet server they are trying to communicate with.

This organization works well with a single NAT IP trying to begin networking with various Internet addresses.

Fresh connections originating from the Internet to the public IP address of the router or firewall meet hiccups. The gateway does not have a means of determining which of the many LAN PCs behind are meant to take the transmitted data because the mapping stated earlier does not occur beforehand. In situations like these data is ordinarily thrown away or dropped.

Port forwarding is a technique of countering this. For instance, you can set up your Internet gateway to forward all web traffic or TCP port 80 traffic destined to the outside NAT IP to be instinctively transmitted to a specific server on the internal network.

Port forwarding is commonly used for website hosting.

Allocation of IP Addresses using DHCP

A protocol that automates IP address allocation, subnet masks default routers and other IP parameters are known as the Dynamic Host Configuration Protocol (DHCP).

Normally the allocation happens when the installed DHCP device boots and recovers network connectivity. The DHCP client sends a demand or request to a locally connected network for a reply from a DHCP server. The DHCP server responds to a query with the IP address, the subnetwork mask, DNS server IP address, and the default gateway details for the user PC..

The IP address would normally terminate after a standard time, when a fresh address from the server's allocated list of addresses will be renegotiated from the DHCP user and network. Thus, it is more complicated to configure firewall rules for accessing devices that obtain their IP addresses from DHCP because remote IP addresses differ from time to time. Perhaps for a single TCP / UDP port you will have to allow access to the whole remote DHCP subnet.

Many routers or firewalls in the local network are built as DHCP servers at the manufacturer. If your Linux box has a static IP address, you could transform it into a DHCP server too.

Physical and Data Link Layers

The TCP/IP protocol suite can be entirely fascinating, but an understanding of these two layers of the OSI model is critical also, since fundamental communication would be difficult without them.

We have numerous standards that describe the physical, electrical, and error-control approaches in data communication. The most prominent in campus and local area networks is Ethernet, which can be accessed at different speeds in a range of network cables, but the technique of data transmission and error correction is the same in both.

Ethernet was mostly used in a configuration where the same Ethernet cable was used by each device in a network location. When broadcasting, machines would wait until the path was clear. You would then return the details by matching what you wanted to send with what you sent to the cable, as a way of error detection. If any discrepancies between the two are found by math correlation and cyclical redundancy test (CRC), the server assumed that it exchanged information with another client on the cable concurrently. It would wait a bit arbitrarily and transmit at some later point if the path became open.

A technique called carrier sense multiple access or CSMA transmits data only after first determining whether the cable or medium between multiple devices has the right signaling levels. The potential to spot garbling is called collision detection or CD owing to overlapping data transfers, also known as collisions.

Connected devices are currently mostly connected via a dedicated cable, exploiting extra powerful hardware capable of concurrently transmitting and receiving minus interferences, thus making it more trustworthy and naturally faster than its predecessor versions. The original Ethernet standard had a speed of 10 Mbps; the most recent versions can handle up to 100Gbps!.

We have the 802.11 specifications outlining numerous wireless networking technologies as an illustration of universally used layer 1 and 2 elements of the OSI reference model. The other parts of these layers are DSL, cable modem standards and T1 circuits.

The ensuing sections are a succinct discussion of the many physical and data link layer fundamentals and how devices that use these layers operate to connect the computers in our LAN and over the Internet.

Network Equipment

Up until now we have only introduced the theory of OSI reference model's first two layers. We will be covering their implementation in the ensuing section.

Network Interface Cards

Network devices are manufactured with an adapter called a network interface card also called a NIC. Presently, the standard two types of adapters used are Ethernet and wireless ethernet adapter cards in the local area networking.

The Meaning of the NIC Link Light

The NIC link light indicates that the network adapter has positively sensed a device on the further end of the cable. This signifies that you are operating using an appropriate type of network cable and that both devices have negotiated the transmission duplex correctly at both ends.

Half and Full Duplex

In transmission media, we have half and full-duplex medium. Firstly, full-duplex medium has the ability to have concurrent transmission and reception of data. Mostly, half-duplex medium can transmit data in both directions, but does it in one direction at a time.

Ethernet medium operating in full-duplex mode uses independent pairs of wires for transmission and receiving of network data so that we remove interference between incoming data and outgoing data flows.

All the networking medium operating on half-duplex makes use of the same pairs of wires for both sending and delivery of data flows. Devices intending to send their data wait for their opportunity to send until the medium is not transmitting anything. Methods for error-detection and data-retransmission guarantee that the transmitted data get to their target destination accurately. This is purposely intended to remedy data corruption which is a result of collisions when several pieces of networked equipment start communicating simultaneously.

A noble resemblance of full-duplex communications is the telephone conversation, in which everyone on the telephone call is able to speak concurrently. Walkie-talkies are a perfect illustration of half-duplex in which both parties wait till the other party is finished before they can speak.

Duplex mismatches where one end has half-duplex and the other end has full-duplex, resulting in low data transfer speeds and high error levels.

The best contemporary network interface cards now are capable of auto-negotiating their medium duplex with the other device. Most Linux servers are capable of duplex automatic negotiation.

Physical Hardware Address

The computer device hardware address often referred to as the Media Access Control or MAC address can be linked to the serial number of the network interface card. That IP packet sent from your Network Interface adapter is bundled within an Ethernet frame utilizing MAC addresses to direct traffic on your local network.

Consequently, MAC addresses are only applicable to local area networks and Layer 2 of the OSI reference model. When IP packets pass through the Network, they use the origin and destination Internet Protocol addresses that stay the same, but the MAC addresses are forwarded by each router across the Internet through the Address Resolution Protocol known as the ARP in short.

ARPing and Hardware Addressing

We use the Address Resolution Protocol to connect MAC addresses to their corresponding IP addresses in the networking environment. When a client wants to connect with another server the following steps will be taken:

1. Initially, the server queries its routing table to establish which Layer 3 router provisions the next hop to the target network

2. When the server finds an entry in the routing table about a router, assuming the router has 10.1.1.1 IP address. The Linux server then inspects the Address Resolution Protocol (ARP) table to find a mapping of the network interface card's MAC address to the above IP Address. This is done to ensure that the packet is sent to the right router for internetwork transmission.

3. If we have a mapping ARP entry, the server then transfers the IP packet to the Router with IP address 10.1.1.1 and ask the network card to encapsulate the packet in a frame for the router's MAC address.

4. If we do not have an ARP mapping in the ARP table, the Kali Linux server should make an ARP request so that the router with IP address 10.1.1.1 responds with its MAC address so that the packet delivery can be made. The packet is channeled when a reply is obtained and the ARP table is updated with the new MAC address..

5. When the routers or gateways in the channel collects the message, it takes out of the Ethernet frame the IP packet, leaving the MAC details instead. It then analyses the target IP address in the packet and uses its routing table to establish the next router's IP address on the path to that target..

6. The router instead uses the ARP protocol to get this next stage router's MAC address. Then it re-encapsulates the packet with the new MAC address in an Ethernet frame and transfers it to the next-hop router. This cycle of relaying proceeds until the packet hits the target machine.

7. A similar process happens when the origin server is on the same network as the destination server The table of the ARP is being examined. If there are no open entries, an ARP query may request the MAC address from the endpoint server Once a reply has been confirmed, the packet will be sent and the ARP table will be revised with the new MAC address.

8. Unless it has an entry in its ARP table for the next path, the Kali Linux server will not transfer the information to its intended destination. If this is not the case, the program that wants to connect may report an error over time and space.

9. As can be anticipated, on the locally connected network, the ARP table comprises only the machine MAC addresses. ARP entries are not binding and will be discarded according to the operating system used after a fixed period of time.

Network Equipment

There are mainly two types of networking device types; the Data Communications Equipment abbreviated as the DCE which is intended to serve as the default communications trail; and the Data Terminal Equipment abbreviated DTE that acts as the origin or destination of the data transmitted.

Network Terminal Equipment

Originally known as Data Terminal Equipment are computer devices that are deployed in remote sites and departments where they are directly connected to modems. Such pieces of equipment do not have any processing power and therefore only act as a combination of screen/keyboard for processing information.

Most PCs have now wired their COM or Ethernet ports as if they were linked to a modem or other type of a network-only system.

Data Communications Equipment

Data communication equipment, abbreviated DCE, is computer equipment used for establishing, maintaining and terminating bidirectional communication sessions. To convert transmission signals, the DCE is connected with the Data Terminal (DTE) and Data Transmission Circuits (DTC).

In contrast, data exchange devices may be known by IT suppliers as data circuit termination devices and data carrier devices.

Types of Communication Cables

In networking, we need straight-through cables when we are connecting disparate device types, for instance connection between DCE and DTE types of equipment uses a straight-through cables. Cross-over cables are used for the interconnection of devices that belong to the same group, like Switch to Switch or computer to computer connections.

We have equipment makers who design their equipment in such a way that they have delineated between ports. Some ports are made as either DTE or DCE. Nevertheless, most modern suppliers and equipment manufacturers design equipment that automatically moves between DTE and DCE. Crossover cables are also known as null modem cables and straight-through cables are called ethernet cables.

Communication Cables

Link-type	Type of Cable
Laptop to Laptop	Null modem cable
Layer 2 Hub to Hub	Null modem cable
Switch connects to Switch	Null modem cable
Laptop to Router	Straight Through
Server to Hub	Straight Through
Server to Switch	Straight Through

Multiport Repeater or Hub

A network repeater is a layer 2 device, used to inter-connect one or more machines in a local segment of a network to permit intercommunication between them.

There are very few advancements for network hubs and therefore no traffic regulations. Most communication devices interconnected via hubs will chat concurrently if they are linked as the signal can be sent via broadcasts to all of the devices interlinked via network repeater also known as the hub. If transmission collisions happen, machines inter-linked through a network hub must attempt anew when there are conflicts in the communication channel after a random period of time. Ethernet modules should be set to half-duplex for these reasons when connected to hubs.

Layer 2 Ethernet Switch

In networking we have devices that operate at the OSI layer 2 which are called a switch. Ethernet switches are just high-speed machine which accepts incoming data segments and diverts them over the Local area network also known as LAN to their target.

Layer 3 Switches

In computer networking, we have devices that interconnect disparate networks, called routers. A router is a Layer 3 device whose sole purpose is to transmit data packets across unique networks. Communication from one network to another network specifically across geographical boundaries.

Routers can also be designed to prevent communication between devices that run on different networks. Inter-network communication is the name given to this interaction that occurs between and across networks. For instance, the connection between two Linux servers on different Local Area Networks trying to interact on TCP port 80 can be rejected and only one is able to classify traffic on the basis of a single packet TCP address.

If you are sending packets across different networks, you need a common routing Internet Protocol address abbreviated to the IP address of each network node to ensure that the router is actually linked to the network-related LAN. The network manager must also specify that links can be sent to the nearby routers and whether this knowledge could in any functional area or routing control be conveyed to the whole router..

Layer 3 switches, commonly known as network routers, typically have only two interfaces that provide internet connectivity through the conversion of a network address or NAT. In other terms, routers serve as entry points to the wider world.

Firewalls

Security Gateways also known as firewalls can be perceived as routing devices with increased traffic control features, not just by port or IP address as routers do. In general, unauthorized efforts to subvert the TCP / IP network can be detected by firewalls. A shortlist of firewall features comprises reducing traffic to a client when too many unsatisfied links are generated to it, constraining traffic to clearly fake IP addresses and NAT, also known as Network Address Translation services. Layer three switches are built to give the negligible amount of inspection to let packets move as fast as possible. Firewalls are used to try to ensure that the information was not subverted as close to the source and destination of packet forwarding as practicable.

Additionally, firewalls may establish an encrypted data route across the Web between two private networks, allowing secure communication with a significantly reduced risk of eavesdropping. Such channels of communication are called Virtual Private Networks, abbreviated as VPNs, and are often used to link satellite offices to company headquarters, and also to allow sales representatives to access confidential pricing information while moving from city to city..

The File Transfer Protocol

File Transfer Protocol, abbreviated FTP, is the best program for file transfer between networked computers. Understanding of the FTP program is particularly vital since FTP is the principal technique of transferring software programs to a Linux system.

There are essentially two FTP types, the first of which is **regular FTP,** which is used chiefly to permit certain users to transfer files to their own operating systems. The distant FTP server prods you to supply a username and password to get entry to the data.

We have the next type of FTP called **anonymous FTP,** which is used principally to permit any distant user to transfer and copy files to their own systems. The user is requested by the remote FTP server for a username, at which stage the user types anonymous or FTP with any valid email address being the key.

It is important to remember that usernames, passwords and information are sent unencrypted across the network, which makes FTP relatively unsafe. As part of the Safe Shell bundle, more safe types like SFTP, known as secure FTP, and SCP, also known as Secure Copy, are accessible.

Chapter Five: Linux Networking

Configuring Network Card in Linux

As a beginner hacker it is critical to know the phases required to configure an Internet Protocol address on your server's Network Interface Card adapter. Linux users may also need to be conversant with the skill to add an additional NIC interface to your server. Network interface setup is a very important skill for all Linux experts.

This book section shows the common processes followed in setting networking on your Server.

What is your IP Address

It is critical for Linux people to know the IP Address of the Server; the command ifconfig -a below displays all the information about a network interface.

[ppeters@rad-srv ~]$ ifconfig -a

ensp0 Link encap:Ethernet HWaddr 00:08:g7:30:34:y8

BROADCAST MULTICAST MTU:1500 Metric:1

RX packets:0 errors:0 dropped:0 overruns:0 frame:0

TX packets:0 errors:0 dropped:0 overruns:0 carrier:0

collisions:0 txqueuelen:100

RX bytes:0 (0.0 b) TX bytes:0 (0.0 b)

Interrupt:11 Base address:0x1820

lo Link encap:Local Loopback

inet addr:127.0.0.1 Mask:255.0.0.0

UP LOOPBACK RUNNING MTU:16436 Metric:1

RX packets:787 errors:0 dropped:0 overruns:0 frame:0

TX packets:787 errors:0 dropped:0 overruns:0 carrier:0

collisions:0 txqueuelen:0

RX bytes:82644 (80.7 Kb) TX bytes:82644 (80.7 Kb)

wlan0 Link encap:Ethernet HWaddr 00:26:45:18:4D:G5

inet addr:172.16.2.200 Bcast:172.16.2.255 Mask:255.255.255.0

UP BROADCAST RUNNING MULTICAST MTU:1500 Metric:1

RX packets:47379 errors:0 dropped:0 overruns:0 frame:0

TX packets:107900 errors:0 dropped:0 overruns:0 carrier:0

RX bytes:4676853 (4.4 Mb) TX bytes:43209032 (41.2 Mb)

Interrupt:11 Memory:c887a000-c887b000

wlan0:0 Link encap:Ethernet HWaddr 00:26:45:18:4D:G5

inet addr:172.16.5.79 Bcast:172.16.5.255 Mask:255.255.255.0

UP BROADCAST RUNNING MULTICAST MTU:1500 Metric:1

Interrupt:11 Memory:c887a000-c887b000

[root@bigboy tmp]#

In this situation, there is no IP address on the ensp0 network gateway, since the VirtualBox is its only NIC by way of a wireless access card wlan0. Adapter wlan0 has a 172.16.2.200 IP address and a 255.255.255.0 subnet mask; you will notice that this control provides the best interrupt data or the PCI bus ID that is used by the device. You notice your NIC card is not operating on a very rare occasion because it has an interrupt and a connection to storage with a network. To get a database of all the interrupt IRQs the system uses, you can access the /proc/interrupts directory contents. The following example demonstrates that no problems arise with each IRQ from 0 to 15 with only one application. ensp0 and ensp1 interface cards, respectively, are used for interrupts of 10 and 5.:

```
[ppeters@rad-srv ~]$ cat /proc/interrupts
        CPU0
  0: 2707402473      XT-PIC  timer
  1:     67       XT-PIC  i8042
  2:      0       XT-PIC  cascade
  5:   411342       XT-PIC  ensp1
  8:      1       XT-PIC  rtc
 10:  1898752       XT-PIC  ensp0
 11:      0       XT-PIC  uhci_hcd
 12:     58       XT-PIC  i8042
 14:  5075806       XT-PIC  ide0
 15:    506       XT-PIC  ide1
NMI:      0
ERR:     43
[ppeters@rad-srv ~]$
```

If there are problems, the Linux documentation for the offending machine may be needed to try and find ways to use a different interrupt or memory I / O position.

Modifying IP Addresses in Linux

The ifconfig statement above showed us that ensp0 interface has no IP address and we can manually assign this ensp0 interface an IP address using the ifconfig command as shown in the statement below.

```
[ppeters@rad-srv ~]$ ifconfig ensp0 172.16.0.1 netmask 255.255.255.0 up
```

At the end of the instruction, the "up" switches on the network interface. You will have to apply this instruction to the /etc/rc.local text file that is running at the start of every restart to make it permanent every time you boot up.

In the /etc/sysconfig/network-scripts tab, Centos Linux often makes life easier with interface configuration setup files. Configuration network interface ensp0 has an ifcfg-ensp0 file and ifcfg-eth1 is used by eth1, and so on. You could paste your IP address in these files, which are then used to set up your NICs automatically when Linux boots. First, the initial network interface has a set Internet address and, secondly, an IP address assignment utilizing DHCP is available.

Network Script Text File in CENTOS

```
[ppeters@rad-srv ~]$ cd /etc/sysconfig/network-scripts

[ppeters@rad-srv network-scripts]# cat ifcfg-ensp0

#

# File: ifcfg-ensp0

#

DEVICE=ensp0

IPADDR=172.16.2.200

NETMASK=255.255.255.0

BOOTPROTO=static

ONBOOT=yes

#

# The following settings are optional

#

BROADCAST=172.16.2.255

NETWORK=172.16.2.0


[ppeters@rad-srv network-scripts]#
```

```
[ppeters@rad-srv tmp]# cd /etc/sysconfig/network-scripts

[ppeters@rad-srv network-scripts]# cat ifcfg-ensp0



#
```

```
# File: ifcfg-ensp0
#
DEVICE=ensp0
BOOTPROTO=dhcp
ONBOOT=yes


[ppeters@rad-srv network-scripts]$
```

As you can see, ensp0 is activated during the Linux system boot process, since the ONBOOT parameter is set to yes or no.

The standard version of CENTOS/Red Hat provides broadcast and network options in the network-scripts text file. This is discretionary.

You have to disable and enable the network card for the modifications you do to take shape, after you have modified the values in the configuration files for the NIC. You can do so using the ifdown and ifup commands:

```
[ppeters@rad-srv network-scripts]$ ifdown ensp0
[ppeters@rad-srv network-scripts]$ ifup ensp0
```

A default gateway for your server to communicate with the internet is required. This was discussed in the previous section..

DHCP and DNS Server Settings

Not only does the DHCP service provide your IP address, but the required DNS server address too. When you use DHCP on a device, make sure to check on the configuration lines of your /etc/resolv.conf file to avoid any conflict..

IP Address Aliasing

You may have found two Wi-Fi interfaces in the previous section titled "Determining your IP Address": wlan0 and wlan0:0. The wlan0:0 interface is a child interface wlan0, a digital sub-interface that is also considered an IP alias. Multiple IP addressing, also known as IP aliasing, is among the most popular way of providing a single NIC with multiple IP addresses. The aliases have the parent-interface-name: X id style, where X is the sub-interface integer of your preference.

The procedure of configuring an IP address alias is identical to the process described for setting an IP address for the main interface in the previous section, "Modifying Your IP Address":

(1)   Ensure that the actual parent interface exists;
(2)   Make sure that no other IP address aliases with this same interface name exist with the identity you want to use.
(3)   This is where we want to generate the wlan0:0 interface
(4)   Generate or configure a virtual interface with just the ifconfig command as shown in the example below

```
[ppeters@rad-srv tmp]$ ifconfig wlan0:0 172.16.2.9 netmask 255.255.255.0 up
```

. The /etc / sysconfig / network-scripts / ifcfg-wlan0:0 configuration file should also be generated so that we automatically manage and control all aliases with ifup and ifdown commands:

```
DEVICE=wlan0:0

ONBOOT=yes

BOOTPROTO=static

IPADDR=172.16.2.9

NETMASK=255.255.255.0
```

The Linux command line instruction to activate and deactivate the IP address aliases is shown below:

```
[ppeters@rad-srv tmp]$ ifup wlan0:0

[ppeters@rad-srv tmp]$ ifdown wlan0:0
```

Please Note: The main network interface termination always shuts down all of its aliases concurrently. Aliases can be disabled independently of all the other alias interfaces. You should be able to ping the new IP alias from other servers on your network after following these four simple configuration steps outlined in the above section.

Chapter Six: Linux Shell Scripting

A shell script is a computer program written in a text file and is intended to be executed on the Linux command line by the Linux shell program; this could be the Bourne Shell, the C Shell, the Korn Shell and lastly the Bourne-Again Shell or bash

The Linux shell is essentially a Linux command-line interpreter. The most basic and standard Linux jobs executed by shell scripts include automation, file management, program execution, and displaying text.

What is a Shell Script?

A Linux shell script has many required and binding concepts that tell the shell ecosystem what needs to be done and when it should be done. Most Linux shell scripts are complicated.

The Linux shell script is a real language of programming like your Java, and comes comprehensively with parameters or variables, program flow control structures, and looping statements. No matter how complex a shell script gets, it is fundamentally a list of Linux shell commands processed consecutively or in sequence.

The shell script below uses the Linux **read** program or utility to take input from the STDIN or keyboard and puts it as the value of the variable called NAME and finally displays it on STDOUT terminal console.

```
#!/bin/bash
# Author: Phillip Peters
#
echo "Please type your name?"
read NAME
echo "Good day, $NAME"
```

Above Script illustrated result:

```
$./test.sh
Please type your name?
Kyrie Peters
Good day, Kyrie Peters
$
```

What is a Linux Shell?

A Linux Shell gives you a command-line terminal interface that is an integration with the Linux kernel beneath. The Linux shell receives user input and executes application programs on the basis of this data input. When a program ends working, the output of the system will be shown.

Shell is an interface of command lines and terminals that helps us to execute our instructions, programs, and shell scripts. There are different shell styles just as Linux operating systems are different. Growing Linux shell form has its own collection of commands and functions.

The Shell Prompt in Linux

The Linux terminal or shell prompt, **$**, which is also called the **command prompt**, is the sign given by the shell that it is taking in commands. Linux Users are allowed to type their commands while the prompt is displayed.

When you are typing on the shell, you signal to the prompt that you want to process what you have typed already by pressing Enter. Whenever the user presses the enter button on their keyboard, the Linux shell reads your input data on the terminal. The direction you want to follow is defined by noting the first word of your output. In Linux a word is a string of characters that are continuous.

Linux Shell Variants

The Linux operating system includes two main categories of command-line shells namely the Bourne shell category with a standard command prompt, the dollar $sign and the C shell category with a percent % symbol as a default prompt symbol. The Bourne shell category is split into firstly the bourne shell, abbreviated sh, followed by the Korn shell, represented by the keyword ksh. The third type of shell under the bourne shell category is called the bourne-again-shell or bash for short, and lastly we have the POSIX shell, abbreviated sh. The C shell category has two prominent subtypes, namely the shell C, abbreviated csh first and the shell TENEX, abbreviated tcsh, Tops C and TENEX.

On most Linux versions, Bourne Shell is usually installed in the /bin/sh directory. The very first shell of Linux was the Bourne shell. That is why Bourne is the shell of choice for several Linux distributions to compose shell scripts in. We will address the most relevant shell concepts of Bourne Shell in this paragraph.

Shell Scripting for Beginners

A shell script is based on a set of commands defined in one execution string. The script with statements, declarations followed by a # sign outlining the actions to be taken, are an example of a well-formed Linux shell script.

In addition to the conditions and tests carried out, we have conditional statements and tests, such as value X is more than value Y. In Linux we have conditional loop statements that allow us to drive massive data volumes, data reading and storage of files, data reading and storage variables and the functionality can be incorporated in Linux script. We do not compile scripts like most languages of programming.

An Example Script

We'll build a shell script text file called example.sh. Notice that we have the.sh extension as our text file suffix when we are writing scripts in all shell environments. Once you write a script for the shell, you must first remind the operating system of the existence of a shell file. We use the shebang format to inform users of the shell script. For example, if you are writing a Bourne shell script, you must begin all your script files with the following characters.

```
#!/bin/sh
```

If you're writing a script for the bash shell you state the script as below:

```
#!/bin/bash
```

The shebang combination of #! is the symbol that tells the Linux system kernel that the following operations are to be performed, either by the Bourne shell or Bourne-Again Shell. This sequence is called a shebang because we have the symbol hash #and the bang! symbol.

Your first position is the shebang line and then insert the commands to build a script containing these commands below:

```
#!/bin/bash

cd ~

pwd
```

Shell Scripting Comments

When you are scripting in the Linux shell, it is always good practice to include comments to describe what your script is doing

```
#!/bin/tcsh


# Script done by James Muswe

# Date: 12th of May 2019

# Script starts below this is just a comment

cd ~

pwd

ls
```

After writing your script in the text file, it is important to save the script and make it executable on the shell terminal. The best way to do this is by using the chmod command as illustrated below.

```
[root@uofzdevops ~]# chmod +x example.sh
```

After changing the mode to executable, the next step is to execute the script in your terminal. That is done as shown below:

```
[root@uofzdevops ~]#./example.sh
```

Upon execution, we will have the following output

```
[root@uofzdevops ~]# vim example.sh

[root@uofzdevops ~]# chmod +x example.sh

[root@uofzdevops ~]# ./example.sh

/root

anaconda-ks.cfg Dockerfile example.sh nginx  Pi-hole  ppeterszw

[root@uofzdevops ~]#
```

Please Note: To run a shell program existing in the current working directory we utilize **./script_name**

Extended Shell Scripts

Linux shell scripts have many essential structures that inform the shell system of what to do and when to do it. We've got more sophisticated Linux shell scripts

The Linux shell scripting is considered a real language of programming that brings with it programming language constructs like variables, conditional and looping statements. Regardless of how complex a script is, it is still only a collection of the sequentially completed sets of commands.

The shell script below **your_age.sh** uses the **read** utility which parses keyboard input and allocates it a value of the variable AGE and displays the result to the STDOUT.

```
#!/bin/bash


# Written by: Daniel Peters
# 5 October 2019


echo "Please enter your Age?"
read AGE
echo "You are $AGE years old"
```

Below we have the result of executing the your_age.sh script

```
[ppeters@uofzdevops ~]$ chmod +x your_age.sh

[ppeters@uofzdevops ~]$ ./your_age.sh

Please enter your Age?

34

You are 34 years old

[ppeters@uofzdevops ~]$
```

Shell Scripting Variables

In this section of the book, we are going to discuss the usage of shell variables in Linux scripting. A variable, also referred to as a parameter, is an alphabetical string to which values are allocated. The value allocated to a variable might be a digit, text, name of a file, equipment, or any data type.

A variable is essentially a pointer to the real data. The Linux shell empowers Linux users to design, assign, and remove variables.

Variable Names

The variable name in shell may include only letters of the alphabet [a to z or A to Z], numerical digits ranging from 0 to 9 and the underscore symbol (_).

Conventionally, shell variables have UPPERCASE names.

Below we have examples of shell Variables:

```
_AMOUNT

SYMBOL_1

VARIABLE_A

VARIABLE_b
```

We cannot use the following symbols **!**, *****, or **–** because the Linux shell ascribes special meaning to them.

Defining Shell Variables

We can define shell variables as illustrated below;

VAR_NAME=VAR_VALUE

```
SURNAME="MUKWESHA"
```

The above illustration states a variable called SURNAME and allots the value "MUKWESHA" to it. These types of parameters are termed **scalar variables**. Scalar parameters are capable of holding a single value only.

Accessing Variable's Value

We prefix the name of the variable or parameter with the dollar sign (**$**) to access its value.

The example script below will access the defined SURNAME variable's value and display it on STDOUT:

```
#!/bin/bash


SURNAME="MUKWESHA"
echo $SURNAME
```

Read-Only Variables

In Linux shell we can mark parameters as read-only through the use of the read-only statement. We are not able to change a read-only variable's value.

The example script below produces an error message while attempting to modify the variable value of AGE:

```
#!/bin/tcsh


AGE=45
readonly AGE
AGE=23
```

The shell script above will give the output below:

```
/bin/tcsh: AGE: This variable is read-only.
```

Variable Unsetting

We are able to delete a variable in the shell script to make sure that the shell stops tracking it through variable unsetting. Once a variable is unset, it is not possible to access the value stored in that variable.

Below is the unset variable syntax to unset;

unset **name_of_variable**

Below we are unsetting the defined variable AMOUNT.

#!/bin/tcsh

AMOUNT=250

unset AMOUNT

echo $AMOUNT

The above sample does not display something to the terminal console. It is not possible to **unset read-only** variables in shell scripting.

Types of Shell Variables

We have mainly the types of variables when a shell is running. The first one is the **Local Variable** which is a variable that is existent inside the present session of the Linux shell. These variables are not available to programs opened or initiated by the shell. These variables are established at the command prompt. Secondly we have what is termed **Environment Variables** which are variables that are accessible to any Linux shell's child processes. Certain applications require these environment variables to function accurately. Ordinarily, shell scripts outline merely those environment parameters required by the applications that it executes.

Lastly, we have **Shell Variables** which are a special parameter usually fixed by the Linux shell; these are mandatory for the shell to function rightly. Several of these parameters are either environment variables or local variables.

Shell Special Variables

This section of the book is a discussion about special shell variables. There are a number of characters mentioned in the previous section which are not allowed for use in naming shell variables. The main reason for this is that those characters are utilized in the naming special shell variables. The special variables are earmarked for use with specific functions.

For instance, the dollar symbol or sign **$** in shell denotes the process ID number, also known as the PID, of the present shell

$echo $$

The statement or command above displays the Process ID of the present shell

156787

The following table shows a number of special variables that you can use in your shell scripts

#	The Variable &the Description
1	**$0** This special variable displays the current script's filename.
2	**$n** These special variables are dependent on the number of arguments with which a script is called. The variable **n** is a non-negative number that

	represents the current argument's position (the initial argument is always $1, the argument that follows is $2 and so on).
3	**$#**
	This displays the argument count supplied to the bash script.
4	**$***
	In Linux we double quote all arguments. If we input two arguments to a bash script, then $* is equal to $1 $2.
5	**$@** We individually put a double quote on all arguments. If a bash script gets two arguments, $@ it results in $1 $2.
6	**$?** This special variable is the exit status of the command executed last.
7	**$$** This special variable above shows the process ID number of the current bash shell. For all bash scripts, $$ details the process ID under which they execute.
8	**$!**
	This variable displays the process ID number of the background command that was last executed.

Shell Command-Line Arguments

The following command-line parameters $1, $2, $3, ...$9 are called positional arguments, with $0 pointing to the actual command, program, shell script, or function and $1, $2, $3, ...$9 as the first, second up to the ninth arguments to the command.

The illustration script below uses numerous special variables associated with the shell.

```
#!/bin/bash


echo "Name of File: $0"

echo "Parameter One: $1"

echo "Parameter Two: $2"

echo "Double Quoted Values: $@"

echo "This Quoted Values: $*"

echo "Aggregate Number of Arguments: $#"
```

Special Parameters $* and $@

There are unique and special parameters that permit reading all the command-line arguments at once. The parameters $*and $@ together will behave the identically unless they are encircled in double-quotes, "".

The two parameters denote the command-line arguments. However, the "$*" special parameter takes the entire list as one argument with spaces between and the "$@" special parameter takes the entire list and separates it into separate arguments.

We can write the shell script as shown below to process an unknown number of command-line arguments with either the $* or $@ special parameters

```
#!/bin/sh


for TOKEN in $*
do
  echo $TOKEN
done
```

Shell Exit Status Variable

The dollar sign and question mark **$?** variable signifies the exit status of the prior command.

Linux Shell Exit status is an arithmetical value outputted by each command upon its conclusion. As a regulation, all successful commands return an exit status of 0, and 1 if failed.

We have some commands that return extra exit statuses for specific intentions. For instance, some commands distinguish amongst the classes of errors and will yield several exit values dependent on the particular type of failure.

Using Arrays in the Shell Script

We are going to initiate a discussion on how to use shell arrays in Linux in this section of the book. All scalar shell variables are able to hold only single values.

Linux Shell provisions a distinctive kind of variable termed an **array variable**. This array variable is able to hold several values simultaneously. Arrays group the sets of variables together. We are able to use a single array variable that holds all the other variables instead of generating a new name for each required variable.

All the naming guidelines we spoke about for Shell Variables are all applicable to array variable naming.

Defining Array Values

The distinction between an array variable and a scalar variable can be described as follows. Suppose you are attempting to portray as a collection of variables the names of different learners. Each of the names is a scalar variable.

```
ARR_NAME01="James"

ARR_NAME02="Peter"

ARR_NAME03="Martin"

ARR_NAME04="Samson"

ARR_NAME05="Linda"
```

To store all the names listed above, we can use a single array. The easiest way to create an array variable is to follow the example below. This enables one of its indices to be assigned a value.

arrayname[index]=value

From above the name of the array is *arrayname*, and the *index* is the index of an item in the array that has to be set, and value is what you want to set for that item.

The example below:

```
ARR_NAME[0]="James "

ARR_NAME[1]="Peter"

ARR_NAME[2]="Martin"

ARR_NAME[3]="Samson"

ARR_NAME[4]="Linda"
```

The syntax of an array initialization, using the **bash** shell, is shown below:

arrayname=(value01 ... valueN)

How to Access an Array's Values

After setting an array variable, you can access it as shown below:

```
${arrayname[index]}
```

The name of the array above is *arrayname*, and the *index* is the index of the value to be processed. Below is the example to access array values:

```
#!/bin/sh


ARR_NAME[0]="James "
ARR_NAME[1]="Peter"
ARR_NAME[2]="Martin"
ARR_NAME[3]="Samson"
ARR_NAME[4]="Linda"
echo "Indice One: ${ARR_NAME[0]}"
echo "Indice Two: ${ARR_NAME[1]}"
```

Below is the result of executing the bash script above:

```
[ppeters@rad-srv ~]$./peters_test.sh
```

Index One: James

Index Two: Peter

Below are the alternatives ways to access arrays:

```
${arrayname[*]}
```

```
${arrayname[@]}
```

The name of the array is **arrayname** . Below is the bash script to illustrate how to access arrays:

```
#!/bin/sh


ARR_NAME[0]="James "
ARR_NAME[1]="Peter"
ARR_NAME[2]="Martin"
ARR_NAME[3]="Samson"
ARR_NAME[4]="Linda"
echo "Our Method One: ${ARR_NAME[*]}"
echo "Our Method Two: ${ARR_NAME[@]}"
```

The result of the bash script:

```
[ppeters@rad-srv ~]$./peters_test.sh
```

Our Method One: James Peter Martin Samson Linda

Shells in Linux, particularly bash, supports a number of operators. This section will discuss in detail the different operators.

In Linux bash shell there are arithmetic, Relational, Boolean, Strings and File Test Operators.

Originally the shell did not have a mechanism to perform arithmetic operations; it used external programs, like **awk** or **expr**.

The example below illustrates how to add two digits:

```
#!/bin/sh


val_add=`expr 5 + 9`
echo "The Total added value is: $val_add"
```

The result of the script above:

The Total added value is: 14

There are a number of points to be considered while performing addition −

- We should have spaces between the operators and the expressions. For instance, 6+9 is incorrect; it should be written as 6 + 9.
- The arithmetic addition expression should be put between backticks' '.

Bash Shell Decision Making

In this section, we are going to discuss bash shell decision-making in Linux. Given two paths in bash shell scripting, there are situations where you need to adopt a single path out of the choice of two. Conditional statements are used to allow your program to make the right decisions and perform the correct actions.

Linux Bash Shell promotes conditional statements based on distinct actions that are used to conduct distinct actions. We have mainly two bash statements used in making decisions:

- The bash **if...else** decision statement
- The bash **case...esac** decision statement

The Bash if...else Decision Statements

For decision making in bash, we use if-else, which can be used to choose an option from a number of given options.

Linux Bash Shell uses the following forms of **if...else** statement:

- if...fi statement
- if...else...fi statement
- if...elif...else...fi statement

In bash, a number of the **if statements** use relational operators to check relations.

Bash Case Statement

The bash case statement, also known as the case...esac statement in bash scripting, is a conditional flow statement used to replace nested if-elif statements.

The case-esac statement is a solid alternative to the multi-level if-then-else-if conditional flow statements. This method of conditional flow enables the user to match a number of values against one variable. Case statements handle multiple branch conditions more efficiently than nested if...elif statements.

We have the case...esac illustration below:

```
case $var_name in

condition01)
    command01
    ...
    ...
    command0N
    ;;

condition02)
    command01
    ...
    ...
    command
    ;;
    *)

esac
```

The **case...esac** statement in bash shell looks very similar to the **switch...case** statement used in traditional programming languages like **Java** or **C++** and **PERL**.

Bash Loop Constructs

Bash scripting utilizes similar programming constructs used in our traditional programming languages like Java and C++. Bash uses loops to take a series of commands and keep executing them until a certain condition. Looping constructs are utilized mainly to automate repetitive and routine tasks in Linux. There are mainly three loop structures used in bash scripting namely; while, until and for loops.

Nesting Loops in Bash

Bash allows the use of loops inside other loops, a process called nesting. In essence a user can put a while loop inside another while loop.

While Loop Nesting

We can place a while loop inside another while loop when we are creating our bash scripts as illustrated below.

Syntax

while commandname01 ; # this is the outer loop

do

  Statement(s) to be executed if commandname01 holds true

while commandname02 ; # this is the inner loop

do

    Statement(s) to be executed if commandname02 holds true

done

Here put Statement(s) to be executed if commandname01 holds true

done

Chapter Seven: Perl Scripting Basics

Scripting languages are a type of lightweight programming language typically authored using structures of high-level programming, making them easy to learn. Although there is no fixed definition of what constitutes a scripting language, some of the common features of these languages are that they are interpreted, type-less languages with native complex types and finally with automated garbage collection.

Interpreted Language

Scripting languages are usually translated by an interpreter into machine-level software during runtime, instead of being compiled before turning into an executable. While this results in a performance hit as each line must be translated on the fly, this allows portability between systems simpler.

Type Less Language

Without needing to specifically define their type, variables can be used to carry any type of data. While this can make it easy to run into design errors, it makes learning the language easier and can improve script readability.

Inbuilt Complex Data Types

Shell scripting just like most programming languages has a number of compound programming data types such as strings, arrays, lists and hashes.

Automated Garbage Collection

Shell scripting language provides an automated garbage collection function which is basically the freeing of system volatile memory used by data. This helps in reducing the probability of system memory leaks during program execution.

Perl, which stands for Practical Extraction Report Language, is a simple scripting language which was fashioned by Larry Wall for the purposes of gathering information from text files and to prepare and publish reports from that collected data and intelligence. It is known as an interpreted language.

Perl is a flexible and ubiquitous language that is found on a varied assortment of PC operating systems because, like Linux, Perl is distributed free of charge. Additionally, Perl is popular as a scripting language among many expert Linux users, hackers and system administrators.

In Linux, any shell, Perl or python *script* is a just lightweight programming source code and the word script is used similarly as simply a program. Scripts are not anything similar to Java, Python and other high-level programming languages that need to be compiled into an intermediary language. All scripting languages like Perl and bash are interpreted languages that are not compiled. The word, script, is used to describe and depict interpreted code that is written in a Linux shell's programming language or in Perl language.

Checking if Perl is Installed

The first step when starting out with Perl scripting in Linux is to check whether Perl is set up and configured on your operating system. We use the which Perl statement to find out as shown below:

We type the command [which Perl]

Linux shell's which utility informs the user whether it has found the program we are searching for in the Linux displayed folders in the environment variable called PATH. We get the example output below in Linux if the Perl program is installed:

We type the statement **/usr/bin/Perl**

When the which utility or command reports that there is no such application in the environment's PATH, this would not necessarily imply that Perl is not installed; this may indicate that you do not have the /usr/bin folder in PATH. It is critical that /usr/bin's is configured in the PATH environment variable; after you have entered the echo $PATH statement you are expected to find out the which command message since this response contains the PATH directories). Use the following command to define PATH if /usr / bin is not in the PATH environment variable:

```
export PATH=$PATH:/usr/bin
```

After the above process, the user should type the **which Perl** statement again on the command line. Getting an error may be a signal that Perl may not be installed on your Kali Linux setup. You can install Perl on Kali Linux using the apt-get install command.

```
apt-get install libpath-tiny-Perl
```

After installation of Perl, you can use the command below to check the version of installed Perl and also determine if it installed.

```
Perl -v
```

The result above informs you of the Perl Version installed in your Kali Linux,

Perl Beginners Script

Perl is a scripting language that has a number of C programming language features, we will begin with an illustration displaying "Greetings, Perl World!! On your terminal console screen. Perl is an interpreted programming language this process can be done directly from the command line if you enter the following statement:

```
Perl -e 'print " Greetings, this is my first Perl Script!\n ";'
```

The Kali Linux system will display the following on the console screen:

```
Greetings, this is my first Perl Script!\n!
```

This Perl command above utilizes the -e switch of the Perl application to pass the Perl script as a command-line parameter to the Perl language interpreter. For instance, the following line comprises the Perl program:

```
print "Greetings, this is my first Perl Script!\n";
```

This line can be easily converted to a Perl script by, simply placing the line in a text file. When writing the text file you always begin with a directive statement to run the Perl program as we do in Linux shell scripts. We should start our text file with the shebang #!/usr/bin/Perl to run the Perl script).

Perl Scripting Steps:

1. The user should use any Linux preferred editor such as vi, nano or emacs, to put the following lines in the file named **greetingworldperl**:

```
#!/usr/bin/Perl
```

```
# This script was written by James 12/10/2019
```

```
# All Perl script comments here
```

```
print "Greetings, this is my first Perl script!\n";
```

2. After saving the above file, change the mode to executable using the command below:

```
[ppeters@rad-srv ~]$ chmod +x greetingworldperl
```

3. The user can execute the Perl script as shown below:

```
[ppeters@rad-srv ~]$ ./greetingworldperl
```

```
Greetings, this is my first Perl script!
```

```
[ppeters@rad-srv ~]$
```

Your first script using Perl scripting language is done. The illustration is your introduction to the world of Perl scripting.

The first Perl script row starts with the shebang #! accompanied by the whole Perl module pathname. If a script's first row starts with the shebang, the Linux shell only strips away the shebang #! Symbol and applies the directory name of the script to the start and executes the code. For instance if your script is named of the script is marked greetingsperl, and your Perl line is written as **#!/usr/bin/Perl/,** Linux shell strips away the shebang (#!) and processes the script as shown below:

[ppeters@rad-srv ~]$ /usr/bin/Perl greetingsperl

On the initial row or line in your Perl text or script file, you can also insert certain Perl options. The -w Perl switch or option is a feature that allows Perl to print warnings in the Perl script about malformed scripting, for instance. Having the -w alternative on the Perl row called by the Perl parser is a good idea. So it is important to use the example script row below as your first section of your scripts in Perl:

[ppeters@rad-srv ~]$ #!/usr/bin/Perl -w

Perl Basic Syntax

Specifically, Perl is freeform as the C programming language since there are no restrictions that occur about where the keyword is put precisely. Generally, Perl scripts or Perl code is saved in text files that have names prefixed with the .pl, without any constraints to the filenames that you use. Each Perl declaration ends in a half-colon (;) just like in the C programming language. A hash sign (#) marks the beginning of a statement, and the Perl language interpreter in Linux does not take into account the remainder of the code that comes after the hash mark as represented with the number sign.

Manipulation of Variables

There is no need to define or declare Perl variables before usage as in other strictly typed programming languages like C. A variable is easy to recognize in the Perl program code because every name of the variable using specialized symbols or characters to differentiate between various variables, the @ text character, symbol $ dollar characters and the percentage symbol %. The parameter type is alluded to by these special symbols or characters.

There are three Perl variable types, namely scalar, array and associative arrays as discussed below:

- The basic data types are scalar variables: integers, floating-point numbers and strings. A dollar symbol $ is put before the scalar parameter in Perl. Here are a few examples:

$max_chars = 256;

$book_title = "Hacker Linux secrets";

- A set or sequence of scalar variables is called an array. An array parameter is prefixed with the at symbol @. The following sets are therefore illustrations of array variable:

@ages = (24, 53, 42, 87);

@colors = ("red", "yellow", "green", "purple");

- Associative arrays are key-value pair sets whereby each key is a string and the value is a scalar parameter. An associative range is represented by a percent symbol % prefixed on a variable name. You may connect a name with a value by using associative arrays. You may store the volume of your disk space in the associative array for each client as shown below:

%space_usage = ("root", 37178, "ppeters", 45557, "kpeters", 75675);

Due to the fact that each variable type has a common prefix with various variable types you may use the same name Thus, the same Perl code can include %disk_usage, @disk_usage and $disk_usage..

Scalar Variables Usage

A single value like an integer or a string can be stored in a scalar variable. The basic data class in Perl is the scalar variable. The name of each scalar starts with a dollar $ symbol. You normally start to use a scalar with an initialization assignment statement, The default value is null, and the default value for the array is a blank number. It is possible to use a variable without initializing it. Use the specified function as follows to see if a scaler is established:

print "Surname is undefined!\n" if !(defined $surname);

When $surname is set, the term (defined $surname) is 1. By using the undef function, you can ' undefine ' a parameter. For instance, the following can be undefined: $surname:

```
undef $surname;
```

The following script initializes and prints several variables: Variables are evaluated by context.:

```
#!/usr/bin/Perl
```

```
$book_name = "Hackers by design";
$count_A = 650;
$count_B = 425;
$total_pages = $count_A + $count_B;


print "The title of the book is $book_name with $total_page pages\n";
```

When you run the preceding Perl program, it produces the following output:

```
Book Name: Hackers by Design -- 1075 pages
```

When the two numerical variables are inserted, their numerical values are used; but when the $total variable is written, the sequence is shown.

With the Perl scripting language when we put double quotation marks "..." around a command or statement then all the parameters in there are checked in sequence. Yet, if you create a list enclosed in single quotes ' ... ', then the Perl interpreter will not join the column. When you type the command below,

```
print 'Title: $book_name -- $total pages\n';
```

enclosing the statement above in single quotes results in Perl displaying the result below:

```
Title: $book_name -- $total pages\n
```

As you may have noticed the statement does not have the cursor moving to the next line.

A default parameter in Perl is the dollar $_ sign attached to the underscore character which is an emphasis character. The default declaration is defined as this unique variable. The Perl parser determines the meaning of this function depending on the context. When the Perl interpreter searches for a specific type of data, $_ maintains a generic request template when the Perl interpreter searches for a particular text pattern.

Perl Scripting Array Data Type

An array data type in Perl is just the scalar collection. The set array syntax or outline begins with the @ tag. Like programming language C, array start indices begin at zero. You may access the set elements via an index. Perl allocates the arrays with adaptive processing.

The text below is an example of usage of arrays in scripting:

```
#!/usr/bin/Perl
```

```
@colors = ("red", "yellow", "green" , "purple");
```

```
$newcolors= @colors;
```

```
print "There are $newcolors colors.\n";
```

```
print "The first color is: $colors[0]\n";
```

The result of running the Perl script above is shown below

```
There are 4 colors.
```

```
The first color is: red
```

The scalar or size of the array is the same total sum of components. If the @ sign is converted to a $ sign and afterward add an index 0 to square brackets, the first component in the array is called. The first part of the @colors

list is called by $colors[0] as the array indices begin at number zero. So the eighth element of @colors array is invoked by typing $colors[7].

We have a total of two scalar types that are special and are linked to the array. The $[parameter is the actual array initialization index and is still standard number zero. The $# array_name scalar has the index value of the final array. So $# is 7 for the @colors array with a total of seven elements.

We can use the command below to list all the components of an array called colors we defined above:

```
print "@colors";
```

```
print "\n"
```

When the Perl interpreter processes the statement above. We get the following result for the @colors array:

```
red yellow green purple
```

Perl Hashes

We are going to discuss Associative arrays which are essentially data structures known as hashes, which seems to be a very useful data structure for Perl language programming. A hash is a way of connecting a value set to a key set ("keys"); a set of key values pairs.

For example, you could use character strings as the index an associative array. The best illustration or sample of an associative array is termed array %ENV that Perl routinely outlines and is a set of environmental variables, which can be accessed with an index with an environmental variable name. This Perl declaration displays to the console screen the present PATH parameter for the environment:

```
[ppeters@rad-srv ~]$ print "PATH = $ENV{PATH}\n";
```

The Perl interpreter will print the recent PATH structure. In addition to indexing the basic arrays, the user must use brackets to catalog hashes as well. Perl has several embedded features like delete and key-value pairs that to permit you to use these hashes data structures.

Predefined Perl Variables

Perl includes several parameters that can provide your custom scripting Perl code with valuable information. Several major predefined variables are listed below:

The @ARGV variable is a set of strings that provides command-line options for the script. The very first option is $ARGV[0], and $ARGV,[1] the second option as we mentioned earlier that arrays indices start at zero.

The predefined variable **%ENV** is an associative array set that contains variables of the Linux system environment. The usage of the environment variable name is a way to get access to this array. The variable **$ENV{HOME** } is therefore the home directory, and **$ENV{PATH** } is the current search path for the control key.

The pre-defined variable **$_** in most Perl functions is the default parameter. Whenever Perl function used without any parameters or arguments, please know that it is probably anticipating the argument in the **$_** predefined variable. The **@_** predefined variable is the set of parameters passed to a Perl subfunction in a Perl script.

The preset variable **$0** is the representative of the file name of the script containing the Perl command. The precast variable **$^V** specifies the version of the Perl language in use on the Linux system, for instance, if Version 6.1.0 is in use, the output of **$^V** will be v6.1.0.

The predefined variable **$<** specifies the Linux system user ID, which is just a unique number that exclusively identifies the user executing the Perl script. This is useful on Linux, since every user has an ID.

The predefined variable **$$** identifies the Perl script's process Identity Number, also known as PID.

And lastly, the **$?** predefined variable is a command that specifies the status of the returned from the last system call.

Perl Expressions and Operators

For combining and evaluating Perl variables, operators are used. Typical arithmetic operators are adding (+), deducting (-), multiplying (*), and dividing (/). Perl and C contain almost the same operator bundle. You end up with expressions if you use operators to merge variables. There is a value for each expression.

Several standard Perl expressions are provided below:

```
temperature < 0

$age == 10

$count + $i

$cars[$i]
```

The above are instances of the comparison method, the arithmetic operator and the array index operator. All terms are the same.

Perl Regular Expressions

You probably know the Grep function, which allows you to search for string patterns of data, if you used Linux (or any version of UNIX) for a while. This is common of Grep to locate all files with any string blaster occurrences or Blaster-on any row of all files with names ending in.c.:

```
cd /usr/src/Linux*/drivers/cdrom

grep "[bB]laster" *.c
```

The commands above produce the output below:

```
sbpcd.c: *      Works with SoundBlaster compatible cards and with "no-sound"

sbpcd.c:      0x230, 1, /* Soundblaster Pro and 16 (default) */

sbpcd.c:      0x250, 1, /* OmniCD default, Soundblaster Pro and 16 */

sbpcd.c:      0x270, 1, /* Soundblaster 16 */

sbpcd.c:      0x290, 1, /* Soundblaster 16 */

sbpcd.c:static const char *str_sb_1 = "soundblaster";

sbpcd.c:static const char *str_sb = "SoundBlaster";

sbpcd.c: *            sbpcd=0x230,SoundBlaster

sbpcd.c:      msg(DBG_INF," LILO boot: ... sbpcd=0x230,SoundBlaster\n");

sjcd.c: * the SoundBlaster/Panasonic style CDROM interface. But today, the
```

As shown above, grep utility above managed to find every incidences of blaster and Blaster in the file system with files with names ending in .c.

The argument of the grep utility "[bB]laster" is considered a standard word, a sequence matching a series of strings. With a limited set of operators and rules you create a regular expression that resembles those for creating mathematical functions. For example, a set of characters within the brackets([...]), corresponds with each character of the group. The regular string "[bB]laster" is therefore series or a set of two strings, as follows:

```
blaster  Blaster
```

Chapter Eight: Installing Kali Linux LAB

This chapter is a Lab to get the user to feel how Kali Linux functions. The Lab will have the beginner hacker gather information using one of the Linux tools in the Kali Linux suite of Tools. We are going to mainly focus on Hydra, Vega, Maltego and the whois service to gather information before setting up our hacks.

Kali Linux is an open-source project sponsored by Offensive Security an international supplier of information security and penetration testing solutions. Offensive Security also funds the attack repository and the free online training, Metasploit Unleashed In addition to Kali Linux.

1. Go to the link http://www.kali.org/downloads/
2. Download a proper version of the Kali Linux image based on your "system type", if it is 32 bit or 64 bit, for example for 64 bit OS you can download **Kali Linux 64 bit ISO**
3. **Using Kali Linux on a Host machine we will use the ISO Image for installation**
4. We need to download and install Oracle VirtualBox from
5. For running Kali Linux in the Oracle VirtualBox, go to the start and type **Oracle VirtualBox** and Start the Application.
6. When the Application is open then Go to the File -> New Virtual Machine and follow the wizard to install the Kali Linux. Go through the process from selecting the Kali Linux ISO Image you downloaded and then Install the Kali Linux and select it from the list at the left side of the page and power it on.
7. After installation you can log in into Kali Linux by typing your root user name and password for example Username: root Password: rootpass.
8. After login, you can open the Kali Linux Applications menu to see all the Categories of Tools on your installation. Go to the Application->Kali Linux to see all the penetration testing tools there.

Kali Linux's Maltego Utility

Kali Linux's Maltego tool is an intelligence and forensic analysis program. Maltego utility is used to gather information and for digital forensic investigations. Maltego provides the information it gathers in a very intuitive and flexible format. We can use the Maltego utility to gather intelligence about a target machine, network or server we may want to hack. The most important step in all hacking is the reconnaissance step which is made to gather the necessary information.

We get to the Maltego utility through the following steps. Firstly Open the Kali Linux Application Menu and Look for Applications then click on "Top Ten Security Tools" and you choose Maltego, and click on it. Alternatively the user can access Maltego utility through the Kali Linux command line interface by typing t Maltego.

The next port of call is that when you open this application, you are then required to register to gain access to this forensic package by means of your email address, if you have not opened Maltego before. After registration you may then login to the platform by means of your registered email address and the password that you set already.

When you open the package you may go to the menu tab and click a circle at the top left corner of the page; Select New to start a new instance of Maltego. When you reach the Maltego palette menu found on the Maltego page's left side, you are required to choose your domain and drag and drop it to the middle of your Maltego page.

After dragging and dropping, you are expected to type the name of the domain in the property view of the domain found at the right side of the Menu. For instance type www.hackersguide.com there. After that please Right-click on the domain and then Choose Run Transform and locate All transforms to website DNS. Then you Right-click on one of the websites and choose Run Transform and find All transforms and point to **Server Technologies Website**.

After the above step you may also Right-click on one of the website results and choose Run Transform; then All transforms and choose to **[To IP Address]**.
The next step is to select the IP address and choose Run Transform then choose all transforms and on the next prompt select Net block using Whois to get the Registrar whois information. The Maltego will show you netblocks

and after that you then Right-click on one of the netblocks and select Run Transform; then go on to choose All transform leading to Location Country Netblock to check the country to which the block of addresses is registered to.

After the above steps, you finally right-click on one of the websites and choose Run Transform, then go on to All transforms then select Mirror: email addresses found and check if you can get any email addresses from the results.

Conclusion

This book is a beginner book that introduces the learner to the world of hacking using the Linux operating system. The book initially eases the reader into what the Linux operating system is and the reasons why hackers prefer the Linux operating system to conduct their work. (Negus, 2015)

The writer went on to introduce the reader to hacking, what it is and the types of hackers that are there in the world, ranging from Black hat to white hat hackers. This distinction of hackers also introduced two terms that are used to mean two things; hackers and crackers. The term hacker in this instance meant an IT expert who uses their expertise to find vulnerabilities and weaknesses in IT systems to make sure that they plug these weaknesses before they are exploited by malicious crackers. Crackers are the opposite of hackers in that they will use the knowledge from system reconnaissance to actually cause damage to IT systems. Crackers essentially enter into systems without authority and cause damage. (Ross, 2017)

The reader is then immersed into the world of Kali Linux, which is the distribution of choice for Linux, security and IT experts to conduct penetration tests, system vulnerability assessments, IT security audits and other types of attacks to systems. The book worked on the types of Penetration tests that are available in the Kali Linux security distribution. The book finally discussed two eminent types of scripting that are critical for any hacker worth their sault; Shell scripting and Perl scripting. The next book in the series will actually look at the actual usage of Kali Linux and two more security distributions. The intermediary book will also look at the more prevalent python scripting, which is now much more used and preferred in hacking than Perl scripting. (Blum & Bresnahan, 2015)

References

http://en.wikipedia.org/wiki/Penetration_test

Blum, R., & Bresnahan, C. (2015). *Linux ® Command Line and Shell Scripting Bible Third Edtion* (3rd ed.). John Wiley & Sons, Inc.

Negus, C. (2015). *Linux ® Bible Ninth Edition* (9th ed.). Wiley.

Ross, A. (2017). *The Ultimate Guide to Linux for everyday people The Ultimate Linux Newbie Guide.* Retrieved from www.linuxnewbieguide.org

CPSIA information can be obtained
at www.ICGtesting.com
Printed in the USA
BVHW051636230621
610214BV00006B/1245

9 789853 821710